Thomas W. Tenbrunsel, a clinical psychologist, is an associate professor and the Director of Foundation Relations at Michigan State University. He has extensive experience in grant writing and proposal evaluation and conducts grantsmanship workshops for university faculty and community agency persons around the country.

THE FUND RAISING RESOURCE MANUAL

THOMAS W. TENBRUNSEL

A SPECTRUM BOOK

PRENTICE-HALL, INC., Englewood Cliffs, New Jersey 07632

Library of Congress Cataloging in Publication Data

Tenbrunsel, Thomas W.
   The fund raising resource manual.

   "A Spectrum Book."
   Includes bibliographies and index.
   1. Fund raising—Handbooks, manuals, etc.   I. Title.
HG177.T46   658.1'522   81-21151
ISBN 0-13-345058-9   AACR2
ISBN 0-13-345041-4 (pbk.)

This Spectrum Book is available to businesses and organizations at a special discount when ordered in large quantities. For information, contact Prentice-Hall, Inc., General Publishing Division, Special Sales, Englewood Cliffs, N. J. 07632.

10   9   8   7   6   5   4   3   2   1

Editorial/production supervision and interior design by Frank Moorman
Page layout by Debra Watson
Cover design by Honi Werner
Manufacturing buyer: Barbara A. Frick

ISBN 0-13-345058-9

ISBN 0-13-345041-4 (PBK.)

PRENTICE-HALL INTERNATIONAL, INC., *London*
PRENCTICE-HALL OF AUSTRALIA PTY. LIMITED, *Sydney*
PRENTICE-HALL OF CANADA, LTD., *Toronto*
PRENTICE-HALL OF INDIA PRIVATE LIMITED, *New Delhi*
PRENTICE-HALL OF JAPAN, INC., *Tokyo*
PRENTICE-HALL OF SOUTHEAST ASIA PTE. LTD., *Singapore*
WHITEHALL BOOKS LIMITED, *Wellington, New Zealand*

CONTENTS

v

PREFACE

The Fund Raising Resource Manual is designed for self-learning and was originally put together as a text for a fund raising course. The *Manual* contains basic how-to techniques on each aspect of fund raising and grantsmanship. It is intended to be useful to both the expert and the novice in the field. In addition to the *Manual*, I am the co-author of *The Participant's Guide to the Grantsmanship Workshop* and a book entitled *Fund-Raising and Grantsmanship: Getting Money From The Community For The Community.*

Each chapter contains an introduction, source materials (charts, examples, and worksheets), a funding strategy portfolio exercise, a bibliography, and a quiz to test your learning. It is necessary to start with Chapters 1 and 2 because they contain basic information that precedes any actual fund raising. However, after studying Chapters 1 and 2, you can proceed to other chapters in any order depending on your preference.

The *Manual* begins with an introductory chapter that helps you to examine your attitude and to look at those processes necessary for successful grantsmanship and fund raising. It stresses the diversification funding strategy for nonprofit organizations. Chapter 2 assists you in setting up or perfecting your organization. Chapters 3 through 8 deal with each of the major funding sources. These chapters stand alone, but the well-rounded grantsperson must be familiar with each of the techniques. Chapter 3 addresses the corporation, the greatest untapped resource for the fund raiser. Chapter 4 focuses on the individual giver, once the greatest supporter of nonprofit organizations and still an important resource in a time of shrinking government spending. Writing the direct mail letter is the topic of Chapter 5. Chapter 6 simplifies the complex process of attaining a government grant. The foundation grant, a small but significant source, is the topic discussed in Chapter 7. Chapter 8 looks at the special event fund raiser: the telethon, the bazaar, the bake sale, and the like.

I acknowledge the following organizations who permitted the use of their materials in *The Fund Raising Resource Manual*: American Association of Fund-Raising Council, The Detroit Producers Association, Dun and Bradstreet, The Foundation Center, Lansing Friends of the Zoo Society, Metropolitan Opera House Guild, Michigan Council on Foundations, Michigan League of Human Services, Michigan State University, National Information Bureau, Standard Rate and Data Service, The Lansing State Journal, The State News, United States Government, The Center of Handicapper Affairs and The Youth Project.

I also wish to thank the following persons for their personal contribution, evaluations, and assistance in preparing *The Fund Raising Resource Manual*: Marian deZeeuw for her persevering assistance, Lou Tornatzky and Michael Yales, and last but not least to Kevin, Brian, and Erin for their encouragement throughout.

To Shirley,
with love and appreciation

Chapter 1

FUND RAISING

This chapter addresses the fund-raising process in general and those aspects of fund raising common to all funding sources. It defines philanthropy and government giving and describes the size and shape of the "given" dollar. You might well find some surprises by examining where the money comes from and to whom it is given.

The first and last word in fund raising and grantsmanship is captured in the saying, "people give to people." Both grantsmanship and fund raising are essentially an interpersonal persuasion process coupled with a lot of hard work researching the funding source. The words *fund raiser* take on new meaning. You must be both a grantsperson and a fund raiser. Grantspersons write proposals and make contacts in Washington; fund raisers cultivate wealthy individuals and design large funding campaigns. It is necessary to know the functions and tasks of both jobs in order to succeed. You have to examine your skills and have a positive attitude. You must become both a writer and a talker to be a fund raiser/grantsperson.

The diversification strategy is introduced in this book. Government, foundations, corporations, individuals, direct mail campaigns, and special fund raising events all represent potential sources of funding for your agency. Whether talking about a small agency or a large organization with a number of small programs, you will need to develop all these funding sources. An example in this chapter compares two organizations with different funding strategies, and you can see which one is most representative of your organization. In today's economy, you cannot be satisfied with a single source of funding. Examine your own program. How many funding sources are you currently using to balance your budget?

The Six-Step Process to Successful Fund Raising is a guide in determining where you are in the funding process. Do not try to skip a step and do not go to the next step until you have completed the previous one. Very often the problem with a fund raising or grants effort is in the inability of the fund raiser to complete steps one through five before writing and submitting a proposal.

The Glossary is provided as a quick and easy reference to the many terms and jargon germane to the fund raising process. It defines and simplifies these terms enough so you can get about the business of "people giving to people."

THE FUND RAISING QUIZ

	Your Estimate
1. How many nonprofit organizations are there in the United States?	_____
2. How much do nonprofit organizations gross annually in the United States?	$_____
3. What percentage of this comes from	
service fees?	%
government?	%
philanthropy?	%
	100%
4. How much philanthropic money was given away	
last year?	$_____
the year before?	$_____
5. What percentage of this came from each of these sources last year?	
individuals	%
bequests	%
foundations	%
corporations	%
	100%

6. What percentage of philanthropic giving went to each of the following categories?

religion _____ %

health _____ %

education _____ %

arts, social, civic, other _____ %

100%

7. How much money do federal governmental agencies give away each year? $_____

8. What percent of their before-tax profits do corporations give away? _____%

PHILANTHROPY

Where the Money Comes From*

	Dollars (in billions)	Percentage of Total
Individuals	$39.93	83.7%
Bequests	$ 2.86	6.0%
Corporations	$ 2.55	5.3%
Foundations	$ 2.40	5.0%
Total Giving	$47.74	100.0%

Where the Money Goes

	Dollars (in billions)	Percentage of Total
Religion	$22.15	46.3%
Education	$ 6.68	14.0%
Health and Hospitals	$ 6.49	13.6%
Social Welfare	$ 4.73	10.0%
Arts and Humanities	$ 2.96	6.2%
Civic and Public	$ 1.36	2.9%
Other	$ 3.37	7.0%
Total	$47.74	100.0%

*Source: *Giving USA: 1981 Annual Report.* New York: American Association of Fund-Raising Counsel, Inc., 1981.

Answers: (1) over 1 million; (2) $150 billion; (3) 33%, 33%, 33%; (4) $48 billion and $43 billion; (5) 85%, 5%, 5%, 5%; (6) 47%, 14%, 14%, 25%; (7) $50+ billion; (8) 1%.

BEFORE YOU BEGIN ...
EXAMINE YOUR ATTITUDE

For years now psychologists have been telling us that people are prone to self-fulfilling prophecies. They say that if you are striving to achieve a goal, but secretly entertain the fear that you'll never make it, your chances of reaching your goal are very slim. On the other hand, if you start with a positive attitude, your chances of succeeding are always better.

In terms of fund raising projects, many fund raisers do not discuss how their attitude toward fund raising affects their success rate with funding agencies. Often grant seekers get depressed and discouraged by the amount of competition they face; they tend to adopt roles toward solicitation that work against them when they look for funding. The ideal role to adopt is that of the trustee. As a fund raiser/grantsperson, you are entrusted by others to carry out their wishes, and you must live up to this role.

A fund raiser must possess two basic skills: You must be a writer and you must be a talker. Most of us are not both. If you are, move on to the next section. If you are not, then use the skill you have and hire the other, while you train at being proficient at both.

As a grant seeker, if you want to win grants consistently, you must project a positive attitude. Think positively, talk positively, become a writer, and work hard. You must regard your work as a profession.

FUNDING STRATEGIES

A Comparison of Two Organizations

	Program A	Program B
Year 0	A mission A small group of interested people.	A mission A small group of interested people.
Year 1	Community grant Hire staff	Community grant Hire staff Small gift from wealthiest board member received Auction fund raiser

4

	Program A	*Program B*
Year 2	Community grant Direct mail solicitation	Community grant Gifts from individuals Annual auction fund raiser Proposal sent to foundation which is rejected
Year 3	Community grant Direct mail solicitation Split into two groups over goals of organization	Community grant Unsolicited gifts from individuals Annual auction fund raiser Small seed grant from foundation to expand services Identification and cultivation of government and corporate funding sources Newsletters to members
	10% cut in community grant because of effects of recession on payroll deduction	
Year 4	Community grant Direct mail solicitation Proposal sent to government which is rejected Reduction in services by 10% to offset cut in grant	Community grant Annual auction fund raiser Emergency fund raiser—casino night to offset budget cuts Newsletter appeal and gifts from individuals and members Foundation grant continued Receive government feasibility grant
Year 5	Community grant Receive 3-year government grant Return services to year 3 level Direct mail dropped	Drop community grant Foundation grant ended Casino night becomes regular yearly event Unsolicited gifts from individuals Receive 3-year government operational grant Receive corporate seed grant to expand program Start direct mail to members
Year 6	Community grant Government grant continued Second government grant received to add new program outside of organization's mission	Casino night Unsolicited gifts from individuals Government operational grant continued Receive second government grant to add new program Broaden direct mail to include other than members Receive 2-year grant from major foundation Plan for building campaign

	Program A	Program B
Year 7	Same as year 6	Sam as year 6 plus: Receive government training grant
	Cut in federal spending	
Year 8	Community grant Government grant I terminated Government grant II continued Name of organization changes	Casino night Government grant I terminated Government grants II and III continued Direct mail solicitation Foundation grant ended Director solicits gifts from wealthy individuals Building campaign delayed Grant from major foundation turned down because outside of organization's mission
Year 9	Community grant Government grant II extended	Same as year 8 plus: Receive 3-year government grant Receive corporate gift Receive two small foundation grants
Year 10	Community grant Return to year 1	Continue casino night, government grants, foundation grants, corporate gifts, direct mail Hire director of development Begin building campaign Begin planned giving program

THE SIX-STEP PROCESS TO SUCCESSFUL FUND RAISING

Step 1: Identify your organization's charge, mission, and goals for the current year.

Step 2: Determine your need for outside funding.

Step 3: Obtain tacit approval from your organization to pursue outside funds for a specific project.

Step 4: Identify granting agencies who are likely prospects.

Step 5: Cultivate these granting agencies and select the most likely prospect.

Step 6: Ask for the gift. Write the proposal matching the needs of your organization to the priorities of the selected granting agency.

GLOSSARY

A-95 review   Boards set up within localities to screen federal funding applications for conformity and duplication.

abstract   See *executive summary.*

Accounting Aid Society   Begun in Detroit by Cook and LeDuc. These agencies provide accounting services to nonprofit organizations. See also *Management Service Organization.*

appropriated funds   Dollars approved by Congress which can then be spent by the executive branch on authorized programs.

approved but not funded   This is one of the things that can happen to your proposal following review by the funding agency. You need to determine if and when you should reapply.

authorized funds   Funds available as a result of legislation which creates a program and an upper limit of dollars to be spent by the government on the program. Often programs will receive a significantly higher authorized amount than that appropriated.

bequest   A gift effective upon a person's demise.

challenge gift   A gift or grant from a government foundation or corporate source which requires that it be matched by the recipient organization.

contract   An agreement between the funding agency and the recipient to deliver certain specified goods or services. Bids for federal contracts are published in *The Commerce Business Daily.*

corporate proposal   See *letter proposal.*

direct costs   Costs in your grant budget attributable to items such as personnel, supplies and services, travel, and so on. See also *indirect costs.*

discretionary funds   Funds at the disposal of the secretary of a department; a possible source of money for a project that is approved but not funded.

diversified funding strategy   The use of all possible sources of funding, including corporations, individuals, direct mail solicitation, government, foundations, and special event fund raisers.

donor   One who gives cash or goods and services to a nonprofit organization.

evaluation   A means of objectively determining the success of a program. Both formative (did the process or program take place as scheduled?) and summative (did it do what was claimed?) are necessary forms of evaluation.

executive summary   A one-page outline of a project to be used in the initial approach to a funding agency or to accompany a formal proposal. Also referred to as an *abstract*.

formula grant   A means of distributing federal grant monies to states or localities on the basis of population, poverty, or geographical factors.

foundation   A legal organization which exists to receive money and make grants.

Foundation Center   An organization sponsored by some major foundations in the United States to compile, maintain, print, and distribute information on foundations. The Foundation Center headquartered in New York maintains regional collections in libraries throughout the country.

fund raising   The process of obtaining funds for nonprofit organizations from individuals, corporations, foundations, and government. Fund raising includes grantsmanship as well.

fund raising pyramid   A structured plan for identifying and placing individual givers at the appropriate giving level before beginning one's campaign.

funding cycle   The time period specified by a funding source in which it will receive proposals (usually on or before a deadline), review them, and make decisions as to which ones to fund. The average cycle is about three months.

funding source   Any organization or agency or individual which gives to nonprofit organizations. The major funding sources are government, foundations, corporations, and individuals who give directly, through the mail, or at a special event fund raiser.

funny money period   Time period toward the end of the federal fiscal year when a surplus of uncommitted dollars exists and federal agencies seek new projects to fund before the money returns to the general fund.

giving history   An itemized listing of who, what, and how much of gifts and grants of a funding source, used to determine the philanthropic interests of the source.

grant   A "no strings attached" gift from a corporation, foundation, or government source to accomplish agreed-upon objectives.

grantsmanship   The skill of raising money for nonprofit organizations by identifying and cultivating funding agencies and writing proposals.

host organization The organization which agrees to lend support— usually space, equipment, or staff—to the organization applying for a grant.

house list A list of those individuals who have responded positively to your organization through membership or an initial mailing. See also *prospect list*.

in-kind match or *in-kind donation* Something other than cash which is received by a nonprofit organization or figured into a grant budget.

indirect costs or *overhead* Costs not included in a budget as direct costs which go to maintenance, utilities, and equipment. You would contact the appropriate government office of management and budget to establish an indirect cost rate for your nonprofit organization (NPO).

IRS 501 (c)(3) Section of the Internal Revenue Service tax code indicating tax exempt, tax deductible status of an organization. That is, a person or organization can give to this type of nonprofit organization and claim the gift as a tax deduction.

joint-funding Often a government or foundation will suggest coordinated funding from more than one funding agency or source.

legal aid societies These organizations often provide legal assistance to community grassroots organizations.

letter proposal A three- to five-page letter submitted to a corporation or small foundation spelling out the terms of a grant.

loan An alternative to an outright gift, grant, or contract as a source of funds. The federal government has any number of loan and loan guarantee programs available.

Management Service Organization (MSO) These organizations provide management services to nonprofit organizations.

matching funds Those dollars figured into a grant budget either as a requirement of the funding agency (required match) or to show the commitment of the grantee organization.

needs assessment A means of documenting a perceived need in the community with data gathered through a number of formalized techniques and methods.

NPO A nonprofit organization is a legal corporation with a board of directors and bylaws. It does not pay profits. It exists usually for some charitable, religious, educational, scientific, or civic purpose.

old boy network Both in grantsmanship and fund raising what still counts most is who knows whom. The old boys network tends to exclude newcomers to the grants process.

overhead See *indirect costs*.

peer review   Review by your professional peers. This process is most commonly used by government agencies in making decisions on grant proposals.

philanthropy   giving of gifts to nonprofit organizations.

planned giving   When an organization is well established and has obtained a degree of longevity, it should begin to solicit planned gifts from individuals in the form of large gifts spread over several years: estate giving, wills, memorial gifts, gifts of insurance, and so on.

PR   Public relations. Public relations is fund raising; the two go hand in hand.

pre-proposal   Some government agencies and foundations are making initial screening decisions based on material presented in a shortened preproposal format. They then usually ask for the full proposal for a final review.

priorities   Those interests which you must determine by cultivating a funding source before submitting a formal request; criteria by which funding agencies make funding decisions.

proposal   A formalized written document which contains descriptive information on needs, objectives, methods, evaluations, and budget of a project for which funds are being requested.

prospect list   Contains names and addresses of potential givers based on demographic or special interests. It is used for the initial mailing in a direct mail campaign. See also *house list*.

restricted gift   A gift, the purpose of which is clearly specified.

RFP (Request for Proposal)   A solicited proposal from a government source.

seed money   Most foundations and corporations prefer to provide smaller start-up funds to projects which will then become self-sustaining or find other means of funding support. In this way, they increase the effectiveness of their limited funding capabilities.

site visit   Once your proposal has been approved, the next step is often a visit from the funding agency to your organization.

solicited proposal   See RFP.

tax deductible   Status determined by the IRS tax code which qualifies an organization to receive gifts from individuals or organizations which in turn claim the gifts as tax deductions.

tax exempt   Status of the IRS tax code which exempts a nonprofit agency from paying certain taxes. Most states have comparable tax codes, but one must apply; it is not automatic.

technical assistance   Besides grants, contracts, and loans, a nonprofit organization can receive valuable technical assistance from a government or corporate source.

unrestricted funds   Funds which may be spent by your organization as it sees fit. Popular sources of unrestricted funds are indirect costs, special event fund raisers, and individual gifts.

unsolicited proposal   A proposal for which there is no formal request. Many government agencies fund unsolicited proposals.

FUNDING STRATEGY PORTFOLIO

The intent of this exercise is to give you experience in a funding project and to move you along the crucial first step of getting started. Toward the end of each chapter, you will find a Funding Strategy Portfolio exercise based on material presented in that chapter. Thus a complete portfolio will contain sections on your organization, corporate giving, individual giving, direct mail, government funding, foundations, and special event fund raisers. You are encouraged to develop your portfolio for an actual project within your organization, or you may choose to develop a simulated project.

In each portfolio exercise, you will be expected to do the work that would be required in an actual fund raising effort. This might include gathering and listing of information on funding sources, phoning the contact person, planning a presentation to the funding agency, writing a proposal letter, developing a direct mail package, and so on. Set yourself a deadline and stick to it. The portfolio should be neat, attractive, exciting, with appropriate grammar, punctuation, and spelling, and typed and bound in a useful and presentable manner. It may be helpful to use a three-hole punch binder to organize your portfolio.

The completed Funding Strategy Portfolio will be a thirty- to fifty-page product to be used by your organization in carrying out its total funding needs. Include a cover letter explaining the portfolio and its contents to anyone who might review it. The portfolio should also contain a table of contents and an abstract, or executive summary, of the organizational project(s) for which it is intended. It may be helpful to record those individuals who worked on specific aspects of the portfolio so that the reviewer can contact them if she or he so desires.

BIBLIOGRAPHY

ANDREW, F. EMERSON. *Philanthropy in the United States: History and Structure.* The Foundation Center, 888 7th Avenue, New York, N.Y. 10106, 1978.

Annual Register of Grant Support, 1980-81. Marquis Academic Media, Chicago, Ill. 1980.

BAKAL, CARL. *Charity U.S.A.* New York: New York Times Book Co., Three Park Avenue, New York, N.Y. 10016, 1979.

BARONE, MICHAEL, GRANT UJUFASA, and DOUGLAS MATTHEWS. *Almanac of American Politics.* New York: E. P. Dutton, 1980.

BENNETT, PAUL. *Up Your Accountability—How to Up Your Serviceability and Funding Credibility by Upping Your Accountability.* Taft Products, Inc., 1000 Vermont Avenue, Washington, D.C. 20005, 1973.

BRAKELEY, GEORGE A., JR. *Tested Ways to Successful Fund Raising.* American Management Association, 135 West 50th Street, New York, N.Y. 10020, 1980.

BRODSKY, JEAN. *The Proposals Writer's Swipe File: Twelve Professionally Written Grant Proposals—Prototype of Approaches, Styles, and Structures.* Taft Products, Inc., 1000 Vermont Avenue, Washington, D.C. 20005, 1976.

CARTER, VIRGINIA L., ed. *CASE Annual Fund Ideas: The Best of CASE Currents.* CASE Publications, Box 298, Alexandria, Va. 22314, 1979.

Charitable Giving and Solicitation. Englewood Cliffs, N.J.: Prentice-Hall, Inc., 1981. Looseleaf, up-to-date service on the technical and legal aspects of charitable giving.

Chronicle of Higher Education, The. 1717 Massachusetts Avenue, N.W., Washington, D.C. 20036. Published weekly.

CONRAD, DANIEL L. *The Grants Planner.* The Institute for Fund-Raising, San Francisco, Calif. 1978.

————.*Techniques of Fund-Raising.* Lyle Stuart, Inc., 120 Enterprise Avenue, Secaucus, N.J., 1974.

FLANAGAN, JOAN. *The Grass Roots Fund-Raising Book: How to Raise Money in Your Community.* The Youth Project, 1555 Connecticut Avenue, N.W., Washington, D.C. 20036, 1977.

FLESHCH, RUDOLF. *Art of Readable Writing.* New York: Collier Books, 1949. One of the best books available to help you learn how to write clearly and persuasively.

Foundation News: The Journal of Philanthropy. Foundation News, P.O. Box 783, Chelsea Station, New York, N.Y. 10011. Bimonthly.

Funding Review. 1135 North Garfield, Pocatello, Id. 83204.

Fund-Raising Management. Hoke Communications, 224 7th Street, Garden City, N.Y. 11530. Bimonthly.

GABY, PATRICIA A., and DANIEL M. GABY. *Nonprofit Organization Handbook: A Guide to Fund-Raising, Grants, Lobbying, Membership Building, Publicity, and Public Relations.* Englewood Cliffs,

N.J.: Prentice-Hall, Inc., 1980. Convenient up-to-date loose-leaf format.

Giving U.S.A. Bulletin. American Association of Fund-Raising Council, Inc., 500 5th Avenue, New York, N.Y. 10036. A source book for annual data on philanthropy.

Grantsmanship Center News. The Grantsmanship Center, 1031 South Grand Avenue, Los Angeles, Calif 90015. A good up-to-date source of information.

GREENE, JON S., ed. *Grantsmanship: Money and How to Get It.* Academic Media, Orange, N.Y., 1973.

HALL, MARY. *Developing Skills in Proposal Writing, 2nd edition.* Continuing Education Publications, 1633 S.W. Park, Portland, Or. 97207, 1978. Good practical guide to writing federal proposals; contains many sample federal forms.

HALLER, LEON. *Using Resources: A Practical Guide to Planning and Financial Management of Small Non-Profit Organizations.* Englewood Cliffs, N.J.: Prentice-Hall, Inc., 1981.

HENNESSEY, PAUL, ed. *The Grant Writer's Handbook, 1978-79.* Public Management Institute, 333 Hayes Street, San Francisco, Ca. 94102.

HUTLER, ALBERT A. *Guide to Successful Fund-Raising.* Business Reports, Inc., Larchmont, N.Y. 10538, 1977.

JACQUETTE, F. LEE, and BARBARA L. JACQUETTE. *What Makes a Good Proposal?* The Foundation Center, 888 7th Avenue, New York, N.Y. 10106, 1977.

LEFFERTS, ROBERT. *Getting a Grant in the 1980s: How to Write Successful Grant Proposals, 2nd ed.* Englewood Cliffs, N.J.: Prentice-Hall, Inc., 1982.

MIRKIN, HOWARD R. *The Complete Fund-Raising.* Public Service Materials Center, 355 Lexington Avenue, New York, N.Y. 10017, 1972.

NATIONAL INFORMATION BUREAU, INC., 305 East 45th Street, New York, 10017. Free index of services.

PENDLETON, NEIL. *Fund Raising.* Englewood Cliffs, N.J.: Prentice-Hall, Inc., 1981.

Program Planning and Proposal Writing. Grantsmanship Center Reprint, 1015 West Olympic Boulevard, Los Angeles, Ca. 90015, 1979.

SCHNEITER, PAUL H. *The Art of Asking: A Handbook for Successful Fund-Raising.* New York: Walker and Co., 1978.

SEYMOUR, HAROLD J. *Designs for Fund-Raising: Principles, Patterns, Techniques.* New York: McGraw-Hill, Inc., 1966. A classic.

SHKURKIN, SERGEI. *By Hook or By Crook: A Fund-Raising Manual.* San Pablo, Ca.: V. Shkurkin, 1973.

SMITH, CRAIG W., and ERIC W. SKJEI. *Getting Grants.* New York: Harper & Row, 1980.

TENBRUNSEL, THOMAS W. *The Fund-Raising Handbook*. East Lansing: Michigan State University Press, 1980.

TENBRUNSEL, THOMAS W., LOUIS G. TORNATZKY, and MARIAN W. DE-ZEEUW. *Fund-Raising and Grantsmanship: Getting Money From the Community For the Community*. East Lansing: Michigan State University Press, 1980.

TURNER, ROLAND, ed. *Grants Register, Sixth Edition 1979-81*. New York: St. Martin's Press. Published every two years, it provides current information on individual opportunities for college graduates and young professionals in the arts, sciences, and professions.

UTECH, INGRID. *Stalking the Large Green Grant: A Fund-Raising Manual for Youth Service Agencies*. National Youth Alternative Projects, Washington, D.C., 1976.

WARNER, IRVING R. *The Art of Fund-Raising*. New York: Harper & Row, 1975.

WHITE, VIRGINIA P. *Grants: How to Find Out About Them and What to Do Next*. New York: Plenum Press, 1976.

———.*Grants for the Arts*. New York: Plenum Press, 1980.

WHITE, VIRGINIA, ed. *Grants Magazine*. New York: Plenum Press. Quarterly.

WILSON, WILLIAM K., ed. *Directory of Research Grants*. Phoenix: Oryx Press, 1980. Information organized by academic discipline about grants, contracts, and fellowship support from federal and state governments, foundations, and corporations.

Chapter 2

YOUR ORGANIZATION

Fund raising is predicated on a credible program run in an efficient, businesslike manner addressing a community need. Thus, before you begin a fund raising campaign, your in-house operations must be in order. You must have a well-defined plan of operation which spells out what your organization will be doing and what it will cost. Your organization must function in a businesslike manner, enjoy a credible reputation in the community, be certified legally, and have a well-rounded board of directors.

Your first step as a fund raiser is, therefore, to outline a current operating plan. The plan (preferably written out) should consist of the following:

1. establishment of *need* for your organization's services
2. a clear statement of purpose or *objectives* (solutions to the problem or need)
3. *methods* or activities to be engaged in while meeting the community needs
4. a means of *evaluation*
5. a budget

A simple current operating plan might be as follows:

The records of the local hospitals indicate that there are fifty people in the community who are unable, on a permanent, periodic, or temporary basis, either to buy groceries or to prepare their own meals.

The objective of the program is to make sure that these people are supplied with meals wherever they need them.

The method of evaluating the program is a periodic phone check or house check to ensure that the clients are satisfied with the service.

This, of course, is a fairly straightforward program, and provided it has the support of a hospital or church, plus a number of volunteers, its funding needs can generally be met by a yearly fund raising event.

Your organization should know at all times where it is, and where it is headed. One way to achieve this is by developing a current operating plan. Having a plan will not only increase the coherence of your organization but also aid you in managing. It will also be useful in preparing brochures, answering questions, and of course, filling out grant applications and generating proposals.

Your needs statement must present the facts, not hearsay. It is much more impressive to a funding agency when you state "a survey by our agency showed...." Document your feelings with fact.

Although there are people who will give to any program that is striving for a better tomorrow, most prospective donors prefer one with a more specific purpose. Unfortunately, there are many objectives that sound specific but are actually rather vague. "Addressing the needs of disadvantaged children," "making our city's streets safe," and "creating a healthful environment" all sound like specific objectives, but they are open to a number of different interpretations. "Making our city's streets safe," for example, can mean anything from campaigning for more streetlights to providing escort service.

Methods are those activities which you engage in on a day-by-day, staff-member-by-staff-member basis in order to satisfy program objectives. They answer the question "how?" which is posed by the objectives. Activities need to be carefully itemized because they become your management tool in any current operating plan or proposal.

If you are a neophyte in social science technology, evaluation may seem unnecessarily complicated. Keep in mind that these techniques are primarily designed to give statistical and scientific support to one's feelings, and also to expose the flaws in one's hunches. If your organization can afford it, you might consider obtaining the services of a consultant in this area. However, there are references provided for the reader who must be his or her own consultant. Remember, the more methodologically sound your proposal is, the greater the likelihood that it will get funded.

Your current operating plan (and any subsequent proposals) should follow this diagram:

COMMUNITY NEED → OBJECTIVE → METHODS → EVALUATION → BUDGET

Opportunity	Solution	Activities	Objectivity	Dollars
		Expertise	Accountability	

An objective is always tied directly to an identified need. The activities to carry out that objective must be evaluated, and they cost money. Note that there is a one-to-one relation between needs and methods and between objectives and evaluation. By arranging your plan or proposal in this way, budget is tied directly to activities, which through objectives meet community needs. By identifying gaps in the budget, you will be defining your fund raising efforts. Your fund raising campaign will be aimed at filling these gaps. When this process is followed closely, your position is always a strong, defensible one.

To get started in building or perfecting your organization, you will need to take the time to fill out the NOME$ Worksheet. Everything you do from here on will depend on it. Once you have completed the NOME$ Worksheet and the Budget Worksheet, you should complete the Project Management Worksheet—one per objective. The last will allow you to manage your organization by objectives and identify those gaps which will become the target of your fund raising campaign.

Much work is needed to see that your organization runs in a friendly, courteous, and businesslike fashion. Phones must be answered, letterhead printed, people hired, and correspondence kept up to date. Do you have well-defined personnel policies? Are your fringe benefits attractive? Do you need to seek assistance from the Accounting Aid Society or Management Service Organization (MSO) in your area in setting up a ledger and keeping your books.

You will need to plan a public relations (PR) campaign to carry your message to the community.

Need	Objective	Method	Evaluation	$

NOME$ worksheet. Fill this out for your organization's project(s).

Last and most importantly, you will need to establish fund raising as a separate objective in your current operating plan. You should designate a person responsible and give him or her staff support and a budget with which to work.

BUDGET CHECKLIST

This checklist should be used in developing a *line item budget* to go into your proposal and to use as a management tool in running your organization. A line item budget includes both direct costs and indirect costs as follows:

For each budget item, be sure to indicate whether the total amount is being requested from the funding agency or donated to the project from other sources.

Direct Costs

Personnel

☐ Salary and wages: List the name (where possible) and title of each person on the project, the monthly salary rate, the number of months to be spent on the project, and the percent of time to be devoted to the project. Multiply these together to get the total.

☐ Fringe benefits (employee benefits): Calculated as a percent of salary (usually around 15 to 20 percent). Employee benefits should be itemized (state unemployment insurance, FICA, workman's compensation, health and dental insurance, life and accident insurance, disability, retirement).

☐ Consultants and contractual services: List title of each consultant or contractor you expect to use and the daily rate of pay or total costs of contract.

Non-Personnel Costs

☐ Supplies and services: Consumable supplies, copying, printing, computer costs, mail, phone, insurance, cost of an annual audit, subscriptions, and so on.

☐ Equipment: Lease and purchase of equipment (lease, if possible, then purchase the equipment after the government grant is terminated for only a fraction of the original cost).

☐ Travel: Travel should be broken down into local and out-of-town travel (to funding agency; Washington, D.C.; professional meetings) and should include an amount for meals and lodging.

☐ Space: Include rent, renovation, maintenance, and utilities under space unless you intend to include these in the indirect costs portion of your budget (see below).

Indirect Costs

☐ Every organization should establish an indirect cost rate. These are the costs incurred when the host organization provides building and space, equipment, operation and maintenance, general administration, and services such as a library to the grant project. In order to receive payment for these services, they must be claimed as an indirect cost. The amount of reimbursement is figured as a percentage of the professional salaries portion of the budget. This percentage, usually ranging from 30 to 100 percent, is added to the direct costs to give the total budget. Thus, a budget with $100,000 in professional personnel and $50,000 in nonpersonnel costs with a 35 percent indirect cost rate would total $185,000. Your organization, in conjunction with the government controllers office, determines the indirect cost rate that will be paid. NOTE: Foundations rarely provide for indirect costs.

☐ Things to consider when making out a budget request:

You will need a budget justification for expensive or unusual items. This is documentation why you need the item at the stated amount.

Be sure to request money quarterly in an amount equal to your budget needs.

Matching dollars increases the power of your hard-earned dollars. Therefore, use dollars from other sources to match government dollars and make them go farther.

Indirect costs are unrestricted dollars.

SAMPLE LINE ITEM BUDGET

Self-Help Health Care Center

	Project Years		
	First	*Second*	*Third*
PERSONNEL			
Director—Project		20,000	20,800
Health Educator—1	14,000	14,980	16,028
Health Educator—2		14,000	14,980
ALM Coordinator	6,000(50%)	12,000	12,840
Librarian	6,000(50%)	12,000	12,840
Secretary	9,200	9,624	10,533
Director—Agency (10%)	3,000	3,000	3,000
Sub Total	38,200	85,644	91,021
Plus 12% TOTAL	42,784	95,921	101,943
OFFICE EXPENSES			
Phone	3,000	3,500	4,000
Postage	2,000	2,500	3,000
Copy and Printing	7,000	8,000	9,000
Supplies	2,000	2,250	2,500
Equipment and Furniture	3,000	500	500
TOTAL	17,000	16,750	19,000
OCCUPANCY EXPENSE			
Rent	12,000	12,000	12,000
Renovation	18,000		
TOTAL	30,000	12,000	12,000

A. PERSONNEL: (Total Salaries and Wages, Fringes, Consultants & Contract Ser.)				TOTAL	Requested	Donated
1. Salaries and Wages				1.		
Position	rate/month	X no. mos.	X % time			
a.						
b.						
c.						
d.						
e.						
f.						
g.						
h.						
i.						
j.						
2. Fringes (SUI, FICA, Workman's Compensation, health insurance, disability, retirement, etc.)				2.		
3. Consultants and Contract Services:				3.		
	rate/day	X no. days				

Budget worksheet.

Budget worksheet, cont'd

B.	NON-PERSONNEL COSTS			
4.	Supplies and Services			
	a. Consumable Supplies			
	b. Copying			
	c. Printing			
	d. Computer Costs			
	e. Mail			
	f. Phone			
	g. Insurance			
	h. Audit			
	i. Subscription			
	j.			
	k.			
	l.			
5.	Equipment (purchase price or lease rates)			
	a.			
	b.			
	c.			
	d.			
	e.			
6.	Travel			
	a. Local			
	b. Out-of-Town			
7.	Space (if charged as direct cost)			
	a. Rent			
	b. Maintenance			
	c. Utilities			
C.	TOTAL DIRECT COST (A + B)			
D.	TOTAL INDIRECT COSTS			
E.	TOTAL COSTS (C + D)			

Remarks:

TRAVEL

Travel	3,000	3,000	3,000
Conference Expense	2,000	2,000	2,000
TOTAL	5,000	5,000	5,000

PROGRAM

Medical Equipment	3,500	1,500	1,000
Medical Supplies	3,000	1,500	1,500
Models	5,000	1,000	1,000
Library Books, Units, Subscriptions	5,000	3,000	2,000
Work Study Stipends	2,000	3,000	3,300
Bookkeeping	1,000	1,100	1,200
Insurance	1,000	1,100	1,300
TOTAL	20,500	12,200	11,300
CONSULTANT SERVICES	30,000	15,000	5,000
TOTAL	145,284	156,871	154,247

SAMPLE LEDGER SHEET

Date	Charge	Personnel	Amount Supplies Services	Special	Balance
7/15/79	Balance Forward				$75,000
7/15/79	Rent		$400		74,600
7/15/79	Utilities		250		74,350
7/15/79	Phone		180		74,170
7/31/79	Director's Salary	$1,650			72,520
7/31/79	Secretary's Salary	700			71,820
7/31/79	Social Worker's Salary	1,000			70,820
8/5/79	Postage for Direct Mail Campaign			$65	71,755
8/5/79	Copying Charges for Direct Mail			55	71,700
8/12/79	Office Supplies		30		71,670
8/15/79	Rent		400		71,270
8/25/79	Income from Direct Mail ($450)				71,720

SAMPLE TASK-BASED BUDGET

This is useful in allocating staff time, justifying budget, and managing your organization.

Agency Goal: Community health planning and development for the Tri-County Region.

Objective: To establish a health system plan.

Activity: Workshop inviting health agency leaders from three counties to complete phase 1 of health systems plan—

OBJECTIVE _____

ACTIVITIES	PERSON(S) RESPONSIBLE	TIME LINE CHART (months) 1 2 3 4 5 6 7 8 9 10 11 12	PERSONNEL STAFF DAYS[1] COST[2]	CONSULTANT DAYS COST	NON-PERSONNEL COSTS SUPPLIES & SERVICES	EQUIPMENT	TRAVEL	SPACE[3]	TOTAL	REMARKS
			TOTAL							
			DONATED							
			REQUESTED							

[1] 240 days x number of professional staff = total project days
[2] including salary and fringes
[3] include here if not charged as indirect cost

Project management chart.

OBJECTIVE #1   DESIGN TWO-COMPONENT TRAINING PROGRAM

ACTIVITIES	PERSON(S) RESPONSIBLE	TIME LINE CHART (months) 1–12	PERSONNEL STAFF DAYS[1]	COST[2]	CONSULTANT DAYS	COST	NON-PERSONNEL COSTS SUPPLIES & SERVICES	EQUIP-MENT	TRAVEL	SPACE[3]	TOTAL	REMARKS
1. INTERVIEW STAFF Generate examples case studies, objectives, etc.	Smith Jones Adams Mohr	1—2	4	800					40		$ 840	
2. DEVELOP OBJECTIVES AND CONTENT FOR BOTH PACKAGES	Smith Jones Adams Mohr	2—5	8	1500							$1600	
3. SIGNOFF	2 staff	Δ 5	2	400					30		$ 430	
4. DEVELOP TREATMENTS AND STORYBOARDS FOR BOTH PACKAGES	Jones Mohr	4—8	8	1500			100				$1700	
5. AGENCY SIGNOFF	2 staff	Δ 8	2	400					30		$ 430	
6. DEVELOP GROUP DISCUSSION PROTOCOLS	Smith Adams	5—9	2	400							$ 400	
7. WRITE INSTRUCTOR'S AND TRAINEE'S MANUALS	Smith Jones Adams Mohr	8—12 Δ	4	300			100				$ 900	
TOTALS			30	6000			200		100		$6300	
DONATED												
REQUESTED												

[1]240 days x number of professional staff = total project days

[2]including salary and fringes

[3]include here if not charged as indirect cost

Sample project management chart.

Airway

Breathing

Circulation

+ AMERICAN ✝ LUNG ASSOCIATION
The 'Christmas Seal' People ®

"The College in the Park"

Preventative Medical Services,

Longevity

Examples of logos.

program identification and priority setting. Include scheduling workshop, workshop itself, compiling data, and presentation to board.

Cost: $3,450.

Staff days: 27

Consultant days: 3

YOUR BOARD OF DIRECTORS

The single most important thing you will ever do as a fund raiser is to choose your first board member. Once you do, this person sets the tone for who will come aboard. If they are wealthy you have cleared the way for contacting others for gifts and perhaps secured your first gift.

Public relations:
a letter to the editor.

Your Opinion

Zoo needs friends

To Sue Briggs and others interested in upgrading the Potter Park Zoo, you will be glad to know The Friends of the Zoo Society also shares your concerns for improving facilities. Through the efforts of the Zoo Society, which was organized in 1969, Potter Park has undergone many major improvements including the addition of a farm yard exhibit; a giant land tortoise exhibit; a free roaming area for small animals; new enclosures for the Gibbons, elk, and deer; renovation of the lion house; a duck pond overlook and feeding station; and of course, Bingo, the elephant, and her home.

Our newest major project is the construction of a walk-through aviary — a bird house that will allow visitors to walk through with the birds in free flight around them. Donations from local businesses, civic organizations, and individuals are making this aviary a reality, but more donations are still needed. Aviary ground-breaking will begin this spring. With your help, Ms. Briggs, and others interested in donating time, materials, and dollars to upgrade facilities, we could complete the aviary project and get on with other projects.

Zoo society board members donate time, and 100 percent of our profits over operational expenses go toward Potter Park Zoo improvement. Improvement projects are expensive. For example, we expect the proposed aviary to cost in the vicinity of $30,000 plus donated time, labor, and materials. We'd love to break ground for a new lion facility; however, the current estimated cost is in the area of a million dollars. Though a lion house fund has been set up already, only $1,159.50 has been contributed to date.

The society carries on several fund-raising drives each year. Frankly, we need more participants in our drives — both contributors and workers. The more people involved, the sooner desired goals can be reached.

SUSAN MAXAM
OLGA OVENHOUSE
Friend of the Zoo Society
Lansing

Some people feel that a board of directors should be made up of "grass roots" individuals. Although this ensures that your board will be interested in your organization, I would advise against it, for two reasons. First, and foremost, is that setting up this type of board severely restricts your fund raising possibilities. (Grass roots people are, by definition, relatively poor. It is a well-known fact that people give to people, and that they give to people most like themselves. In other words, the rich give to the rich.) The second reason is that the board that is entirely interested in general policy turns out to be a do-nothing board. Meetings center entirely on discussions of, and arguments over, policy issues, the end result being that often the board simply rubber-stamps what your organization is already doing.

Chances are that your organization already has a board filled with either "community leaders" or "grass roots" individuals. Although you cannot revamp your board in one fell swoop, I suggest that you keep the following sets of individuals in mind as the terms of office of your board members expire:

The Wealthy—At least one member of your board should be the wealthiest and most influential member of your community that you can identify and talk into serving on your board. He or she should generally be asked to serve as board chairman, and possibly as director of fund raising. Your wealthy member will be most useful in soliciting individual and corporate gifts. The chapter on individual giving will provide information on how to locate this type of member.

The Wise—Lawyers, CPA's, businessmen, and university professors fall into this category. You should have one of each to provide you with free legal, financial, and business advice. The university professor should be someone who has had experience in writing formal proposals and getting government and/or foundation grants.

The Workers—The worker member of your board should be someone who can draft and organize volunteers for community fund raising events and direct mail campaigns. This person is generally identified as the "professional volunteer," and she (although I do not intend to perpetuate sexist stereotypes, this person generally is female) should have a wide range of experience in organizing bake sales, church bazaars, luncheons, benefit concerts, and so on.

The Worriers—One or two of your board members should have a firm idea of your organization's goals and overall direction. These members should be able to tell you whether your new program is in keeping with the primary purpose of your organization or whether it is a deviation. Give them a copy of your current operating plan and ask them to review all proposals to funding sources. This will ensure that in "matching your interests to theirs," you do not become an organizational prostitute, ready to provide any service as long as you can get funding for it. Worriers (also known as concerned citizens) come in all shapes and sizes. Try to get one who worries about the actions of your organization, rather than the actions of the universe in general.

The above constitutes the ideal board, both for fund raising and operations. I would strongly urge you to keep these guidelines in mind when setting up or changing your board of directors. A good, mixed pool of talent is the first prerequisite to successful fund raising.

INCORPORATION CHECKLIST

The Incorporation Checklist will help nonprofit organizations incorporate and obtain tax-exempt status.

- ☐ Obtain forms for incorporation of a nonprofit organization and for filing for tax-exempt status in your state from the U.S. Department of Commerce, Secretary of State, or Attorney General's office.
- ☐ Obtain Publication 557, *How to Apply for and Retain Exempt Status for Your Organization,* from the local IRS office. This is a thorough explanation of federal tax-exempt, tax-deductible status.
- ☐ Obtain Package 1023, *Application for Recognition of Exemption,* from the local IRS office.
- ☐ Fill our incorporation and tax forms. Where necessary, obtain assistance from another, similar, nonprofit organization. If in doubt, obtain legal assistance. Make sure all forms are complete. Articles of incorporation generally include
  name of organization
  address

statement of general "charitable, religious, educational, or scientific" purpose and specific purpose of organization
statement of nonprofit intent
statement of what will happen upon dissolution
resident agent and address
three legal age signatures

☐ File your articles of incorporation. You should wait until it is absolutely necessary to file and pay the fee ($35 to $50 excluding legal fees which could run in excess of $400).

☐ Draw up your bylaws in the following format (again use the bylaws of a successful nonprofit group as a guide):

Article I: Name
Article II: Purpose
Article III: Membership
Article IV: Officers
Article V: Election of officers and of office term
Article VI: Duties of officers
Article VII: Meetings
Article VIII: Committees
Article IX: Quorums
Article X: Amendments

☐ Hold your first board meeting.

☐ File for tax-exempt status.

☐ File for tax deductible status IRS 501(c)(3), allowing individuals and corporations to deduct their gifts to your organization from their income tax.

☐ Make note on your annual calendar of the reporting forms you are required to submit as a result of being an exempt nonprofit organization.

FUNDING STRATEGY PORTFOLIO

EXERCISE 1
Fill out the NOME$ Worksheet for your project.

EXERCISE 2
Complete the Budget Worksheet for your project.

EXERCISE 3
Complete a Project Management Chart for each major objective of your project.

Internal Revenue Service   Department of the Treasury
District Director

Date: Employer Identification Number:
                                  52-3860801
                                  Accounting Period Ending:

PROJECT COLUMBIA   December 31st
1401 EDGEWOOD BLVD.   Form 990 Required: X yes _no
LANSING, MI 48910

                                  Contact Teelphone Number:

                                  (313) 226-7330
                                  (Not Toll Free)

Dear Applicant:

    Based on information supplied, and assuming your operations will be as
stated in your application for recognition of exemption, we have determined
you are exempt from Federal income tax under section 501(C)(3) of the
Internal Revenue Code.

    We have further determined that you are not a private foundation with-
in the meaning of section 509(a) of the Code, because you are an organization described in section 509(a)(2).

    If your sources of support, or your purposes, character, or method of
operation change, please let us know so we can consider the effect of the
change on your exempt status and foundation status. Also, you should in-
form us of all changes in your name or address.

    Generally, you are not liable for social security (FICA) taxes unless
you file a waiver of exemption certificate as provided in the Federal Insurance Contributions Act. If you have paid FICA taxes without filing the
waiver, you should contact us. You are not liable for the tax imposed under the Feredal Unemployment Tax Act (FUTA).

    Since you are not a private foundation, you are not subject to the ex-
cise taxes under Chapter 42 of the Code. However, you are not automatically
exempt from other Federal excise taxes. If you have any questions about excise, employment, or other Federal taxes, please let us know.

    Donors may deduct contributions to you as provided in section 170 of
the Code. Bequests, legacies, devises, transfers, or gifts to you or for
your use are deductible for Federal estate and gift tax purposes if they
meet the applicable provisions of sections 2055, 2106, and 2522 of the Code.

    The box checked in the heading of this letter shows whether you must
file Form 990, Return of Organization Exempt from Income Tax. If Yes is
checked, you are required to file Form 990 only if your gross receipts each

                        (over)

P.O. Box 32510, Detroit, MI 48232

year are normally more than $10,000. If a return is required, it must be filed by the 15th day of the fifth month after the end of your annual accounting period. The law imposes a penalty of $10 a day, up to a maximum of $5,000, when a return is filed late, unless there is reasonable cause for the delay.

You are required to file Federal income tax returns unless you are subject to the tax on unrelated business income under section 511 of the Code. If you are subject to this tax, you must file an income tax return on Form 990-T. In this letter, we are not determining whether any of your present or proposed activities are unrelated trade or business as defined in section 513 of the Code.

You need an employer identification number even if you have no employees.

If an employer identification number was not entered on your application, a number will be assigned to you and you will be advised of it. Please use that number on all returns you file and in all correspondence with the Internal Revenue Service.

Because this letter could help resolve any questions about your exempt status and foundation status, you should keep it in your permanent records.

If you have any questions, please contact the person whose name and telephone number are shown in the heading of this letter.

Sincerely yours,

District Director

EXERCISE 4
Evaluate the businesslike image of staffing, personnel policies, phones, accounting and financing, and office behavior in your organization and list those things which need to be changed.

EXERCISE 5
Evaluate the public image (organization's name, logo, stationery, newsletter, media PR) and list recommendations necessary toward implementing a funding campaign.

EXERCISE 6
Evaluate your board of directors.

EXERCISE 7
Draw up or review incorporation papers, bylaws, IRS 501(c)(3) letter, and determine changes necessary before a successful funding strategy can be implemented for your organization.

EXERCISE 8

Identify an ad hoc group within your organization which will be responsible for developing the funding strategy. What one person will be responsible for this group?

EXERCISE 9

Obtain approval from your organization to proceed with a funding strategy taking into account all projects and activities of your organization.

BIBLIOGRAPHY

Accounting, Finance
and Management

Accounting and Financial Reporting. United Way of America, 801 North Fairfax Street, Alexandria, VA 22314, 1974.

BENNETT, PAUL. *Up Your Accountability—How to Up Your Serviceability and Funding Credibility by Upping Your Accountability.* Taft Products, Inc., 1000 Vermont Avenue, Washington, D.C. 20005, 1973.

Budgeting. United Way of America, 801 North Fairfax Street, Alexandria, VA 22314, 1975.

CONNORS, TRACY D., ed. *The Nonprofit Organization Handbook.* New York: McGraw-Hill, Inc., 1980.

COOK, LEWIS, and ROBERT R. LEDUC. "Accounting Aid Society of Metropolitan Detroit." *Foundation News,* November/December 1977.

GABY, PATRICIA A., and DANIEL M. GABY. *Nonprofit Organization Handbook: A Guide to Fund-Raising Grants, Lobbying, Membership Building, Publicity, and Public Relations.* Englewood Cliffs, N.J.: Prentice-Hall, Inc., 1979. Convenient up-to-date loose-leaf format.

GROSS, MALVERN J., JR. *Financial Accounting Guide for Nonprofit Organizations.* New York: John Wiley and Sons, 1979. New edition.

HALLER, LEON. *Using Resources: A Practical Guide to Planning and Financial Management of Small Non-Profit Organizations.* Englewood Cliffs, N.J.: Prentice-Hall, Inc., 1981.

HENKE, EMERSON O. *Accounting for Non-Profit Organizations.* Belmont, Cal.: Wadsworth Publishing Co., 1966.

JONES, O. GARFIELD. *Parliamentary Procedure at a Glance.* New York: Hawthorn Books, Inc., 1932.

National Directory of Nonprofit Management Support Organizations. The Support Center, 1709 New Hampshire Avenue, N.W., Washington, D.C. 20009, 1980.

Tax-Exempt Organizations. Englewood Cliffs, N.J.: Prentice-Hall, Inc., 1981. A monthly looseleaf service with reports, articles, and news items on the latest developments in all types of tax-exempt organizations.

WHITAKER, FRED A. *How to Form Your Own Non-Profit Corporation in One Day: Learn How to Save Money.* Minority Management Institute, 872 69th Avenue, Oakland, Cal. 94621, 1979.

Needs Assessment

DELBECQ, ANDRE L., et al. *Group Techniques for Program Planning: A Guide to the Nominal Group and Delphi Processes.* Glenview, Ill.: Scott Foresman Co., 1975.

SCHWAB, JOHN J., GEORGE J. WARHEIT, EILEEN B. FENNELL, RICHARD STEWART, LARRY POASTER, AUDREY T. WEISS, CHARLES WINDLE, BEATRICE M. ROSEN, HAROLD R. GOLDSMITH, and PHILIP J. SHAMBAUGH. "Needs Assessment Methods for the Community Mental Health Center." *Evaluation,* Vol. 2, No. 2, 1975, 64-76.

WEBB, K., and H. HATRY. *Obtaining Citizen Feedback: The Application of Citizen Surveys to Local Governments.* The Urban Institute, Washington, D.C., 1973.

Obtaining Tax Deductible Status

Application for Recognition of Exemption. IRS Package 1023.

How to Apply for and Retain Exempt Status for Your Organization. IRS Publication 557.

TREUSCH, PAUL E., and NORMAN A. SUGARMAN. *Tax Exempt Charitable Organizations.* American Law Institute, 4025 Chestnut Street, Philadelphia, PA 19104, 1979.

Program Evaluation

The specific measurement of program impact can be approached in two ways. One route is to create one's own questionnaires, inventories, interview schedules, and so on. This is no mean task, and considerations of reliability, internal consistency, and validity are extremely important. The curious but naive reader ought to consult some basic texts before deciding to try it:

ADAMS, S. *Evaluative Research in Corrections: A Practical Guide.* Washington, D.C.: U.S. Department of Justice, 1975.

BONJEAN, C.M., R.J. HILL, and S.D. McLEMORE. *Sociological Measurement: An Inventory of Scales and Indices.* San Francisco: Chandler Publishing Company, 1967.

CAMPBELL, D.T., and J. C. STANLEY. *Experimental and Quasi-Experimental Designs for Research.* Chicago: Rand McNally & Co., 1966.

COMREY, A.L., T. E. BACKER, and C. M. GLASER. *A Sourcebook for Mental Health Measures.* Human Interaction Research Institute, Los Angeles, Cal., 1973.

FAIRWEATHER, G. W., and L. G. TORNATZKY. *Experimental Methods for Social Policy Research.* New York: Pergamon Press, 1977.

HATRY, H., R. E. WINNIE, and D. FISK. *Practical Program Evaluation for State and Local Government Officials.* The Urban Institute, Washington, D.C., 1973.

NUNNALLY, J. *Introduction to Psychological Measurement.* New York: McGraw-Hill, Inc., 1970.

RIVLIN, ALICE M., and P. MICHAEL TIMPAINE, eds. *Ethical and Legal Issues of Social Science Experimentation.* Washington, D.C.: The Brookings Institution, 1975.

WEISS, CAROL H. *Evaluating Action Programs.* Boston: Allyn & Bacon, Inc., 1972.

Setting Program Goals and Objectives

MAGER, ROBERT F. *Preparing Instructional Objectives.* Belmont, Cal.: Fearson Publishers, 1962. A presentation oriented to the lay person.

MORIS, LYNN LYONS, and CAROL TAYLOR FITZ-GIVVON. *How to Deal with Goals and Objectives.* Beverly Hills, Cal.: Sage Publication, 1978.

Standards for Fund Raising

Give But Give Wisely. Council of Better Business Bureaus, Inc., 1150 17th Street, N.W., Washington, D.C. 20036, 1978.

*Notification to Soliciting Organizations....*Council of Better Business Bureaus, Inc., 1150 17th Street, N.W., Washington, D.C. 20036, 1977.

O'ROURKE, HELEN. *Standards for Charitable Solicitation.* Council of Better Business, Inc., 1150 17th Street, N.W., Washington, D.C. 20036, 1978.

Wise Giving Bulletin. National Information Bureau, 419 Park Avenue So., New York, N.Y. 10016, 1979.

Public Relations:
Television, Radio, Newspaper Publicity

BATES, DON. *Communicating and Money-Making: A Guide for Using Public Relations to Improve Fund-Raising Success.* New York: Heladon Press, 1980.

BERNAYS, EDWARD L. *Public Relations.* Norman: University of Oklahoma Press, 1970.

BIEGEL, LEN, and AILEEN LUBIN. *Mediability: A Guide for Non-Profits.* Taft Products, Inc., 1000 Vermont Avenue, Washington, D.C. 20005, 1975.

CUTLIP, SCOTT M., and ALLEN H. CANTER. *Effective Public Relations.* Englewood Cliffs, N.J.: Prentice-Hall, Inc., 1978.

"How Public Relations Can Help Your Fund-Raising Efforts Pay Off." *Grantsmanship Center News,* Issue 30, p. 36.

If You Want Air Time: A Publicity Handbook. Station Services Department, National Association of Broadcasters, 1771 North Street, N.W., Washington, D.C. 20036, 1977. Includes how to approach radio and television, what to ask for, some do's and don'ts, and sample public service announcements.

MARTINES, BARBARA F., and ROBERT WEINER. "The Press Release." *Grantsmanship Center News,* Issue 19, p. 38.

Public Relations and How to Use It. SEDRFE, New York, N.Y. 10001, 1978. Includes the techniques of public relations and suggestions on how to deal with reporters.

RICHMAN, SAUL. *Public Information Handbook for Foundations.* Council on Foundations, 888 7th Avenue, New York, N.Y. 10016, 1973.

Comprehensive bibliographies on public relations materials are available from

Public Relations Society of America, 845 Third Avenue, New York, N.Y. 10022.

Community Mental Health Materials Center, 419 Park Avenue South, New York, N.Y. 10016.

The Public Media Center, 2751 Hyde Street, San Francisco, Cal. 94109.

QUIZ

Answer true or false.

1. Fund raising is predicated on a credible program run in an efficient, businesslike manner.
2. In order to be the recipient of a tax-deductible gift, you must qualify as an IRS 105(3)D organization.
3. Most prospective donors prefer giving to a program with a specific purpose.
4. Nonprofit organizations are restricted by the Internal Revenue Service to cash gifts only.
5. Staff members, rather than board members, should approach individuals and corporations for gifts.
6. Every nonprofit organization should have a current operating plan.
7. The ideal board consists of people with money, people with expertise, people who work hard, and people who worry about the organization.
8. A current operating plan should spell out needs, objectives, methods, evaluation, and budget for the organization.
9. Fund raising should be a budgeted activity in any established nonprofit organization.
10. The more you publicize your organization, the greater the visibility and the better your chances of getting funded.

Answers: (1) T, (2) F, (3) T, (4) F, (5) F, (6) T, (7) T, (8) T, (9) T, (10) T.

Chapter 3

CORPORATE GIVING

Of all the fund raising sources, corporations are truly the untapped resource. They typically give only 1 percent of their before-tax profits to charitable causes when, by law, they can give up to 10 percent. The primary reason for this is that they are not asked, that not enough pressure is placed on them to respond to community needs with their fair share. We have let them off the hook, so to speak, by allowing them to give token gifts.

Undoubtedly the best method of approaching a corporation for a gift is through the old boy network. That is, your board chairman approaches the corporation's president. The second best method is identifying corporations in your geographic area and approaching them yourself. The Six-Step Process to Identifying Corporate Resources will get you started.

Following the procedures outlined in this chapter, you can begin to build your own in-house corporate funding strategy. The Generosity Index is a measure of how generous a company is. It will raise your level of awareness of corporations and help you decide which corporation to approach first.

Corporations don't have to give money away. In fact, they exist to make and retain as much money as possible. Your job as fund raiser is to convince them to give, and you do this by showing them how a gift to your organization is good for their business (*quid pro quo*). It also helps if your program will benefit employees of the corporation, and you must be a tax-deductible nonprofit organization.

Get to know the people who make the decisions for the corporation and its past giving history. Match your interests to theirs. Be prepared to spend many hours in the library, on the phone, and in personal contacts researching the information and cultivating the giver. After the gift has been committed, you will prepare a short letter proposal which will serve as the official

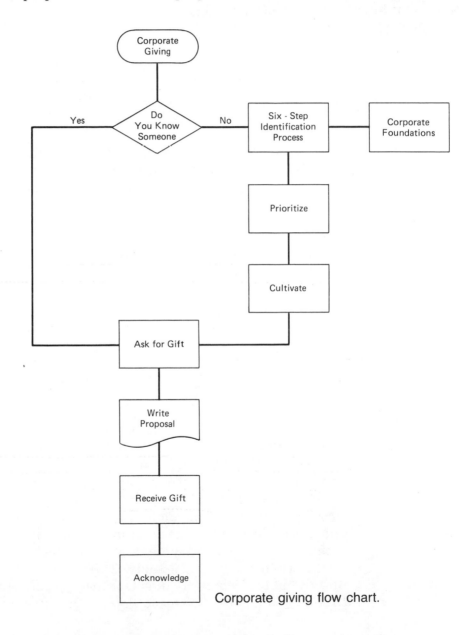

Corporate giving flow chart.

request. Once you have received the gift, you should say thank you with an appropriate acknowledgement.

Some corporations have corporate foundations. Their purpose is to provide a continuous level of giving which is independent of the corporation's fluctuating economy. You should approach both the corporation and its foundation for coordinated giving.

SIX-STEP PROCESS TO IDENTIFYING CORPORATE RESOURCES

Making the List

You will need the following equipment: map, compass, index cards, Rol-a-dex or computer cards, calculator (optional).

STEP 1

Make a list of all the cities in your geographic region within a twenty-five mile radius. You might want to use same county, same area of state, or make special exceptions outside the radius. In large urban areas, you will need to be more selective.

STEP 2

Go to the geographical index ("Businesses Geographically") of the Dun and Bradstreet *Million Dollar Directory*, Vols. I, II, and III. Look up the cities on your list (the geographical index is alphabetical by state), and write the names of the corporations on your index cards (one card for each corporation) in the top left-hand corner. If you are interested only in grants of $1,000 or over, use only Volume I; otherwise, keep your listings from Volume I and Volumes II and III in separate piles. Alphabetize your cards.

STEP 3

Go to the alphabetical listing of corporations ("Businesses Alphabetically"). For each corporation, write the address, phone number, nature of business, and number of employees on the left-hand side under the corporation name. In the top right-hand corner, write the first SIC number (this is the standard industrial classification code, which tells what type of industry the corporation is engaged in). Some corporations have more than one SIC number, but you should write down only the first number given as this is the principal activity. This number is essential for finding out the Generosity Index for that type of corporation. The *Dun and Bradstreet Reference Book of Manufacturers* will give the "Estimated Financial Strength Code" for most businesses. Copy this down for future reference. Now, turn the card over and write down the starred names (these are corporate officers who are also members of the board of directors) and their positions, and the names at the bottom of the list (these are members of the board of directors). You may also want to list the other corporate officers because these will be useful for individual giving.

When you have done this for every corporation, put the cards from Volumes II and III aside (you will come back to them at Step 6).

STEP 4

Now turn to the Generosity Index Chart in this section. The Generosity Index (GI) is the annual charitable contribution divided by the annual net income before taxes. The Internal Revenue Service surveys the contributions of industries by type of industry. A GI has been assigned for each type of major industry. Although this figure is based on the contributions given by *all* corporations in a certain type of industry, and thus cannot be applied to a particular corporation, it will help the fund raiser estimate the amount a particular corporation will be likely to give.

Look up the SIC number on the chart, and write down the GI number on the right-hand side of your card.

STEP 5

Next, you need to determine the corporation's net income before taxes or before tax earnings (BTE). The following sources will give this information:

Standard and Poor's Stock Reports
Standard and Poor's Corporation Records
Moody's Handbook of Common Stocks
Moody's Industrial Manual
Moody's Public Utility Manual
Moody's Bank and Finance Manual
Dun and Bradstreet Visual Records (3 × 5 cards)
Corporate annual reports of all types

Write down the net income before taxes (some references refer to it as net income plus taxes) on the right-hand side of your card under the GI number.

You will probably find that you are left with about nine out of ten corporations for which no BTE is listed in any of the above sources. If this is so, the "Estimated Financial Strength Code" in the *Dun and Bradstreet Reference Book of Manufacturers* will give you a range of asset size for the corporation. You can use 10 percent of this figure as a rough estimate of the BTE. You can also call or write the corporation and request their annual report. The annual report will give before-tax earnings. You should remember that it is the hard-to-reach corporation that is a very good bet for you, and finding a company's BTE is getting to know the company, its personnel, and its potential giving capacities.

Sample corporate directory entry.

Source: *Million Dollar Directory*®, Volume I. Dun's Marketing Services, a company of the Dun & Bradstreet Corporation, Three Century Drive, Parsippany, N.J. 07054

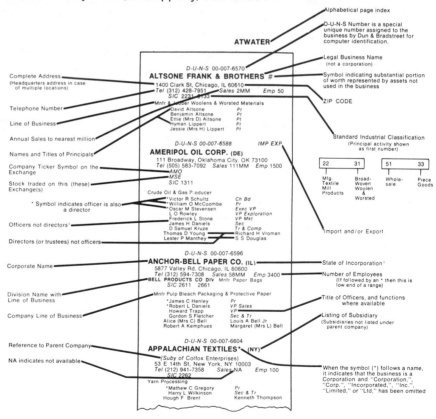

¹Assistant Officers, and Limited Partners are generally not listed. Individuals in charge of Finance, Advertising, Sales, Purchasing and Production may be listed even though not corporate officers.

²Names of National Banks are followed by the notation (Natl); Names of State Banks by State abbreviation.

STEP 6

Multiply the before-tax earnings (BTE) figure by the Generosity Index (GI) figure, and write down the estimated maximum gift on the right-hand side. If you have been unable to obtain the BTE, then indicate your best guess or that of your friendly banker. This estimated maximum gift for you will be reduced in size proportional to the number of other organizations receiving gifts from that corporation in any given year.

For corporations listed in Volumes II and III of the *Million Dollar Directory*, the estimated maximum gift will be $500 to $1,000. Either write this down on each card, or rubber band your cards together and note that these corporations cannot be expected to give more than $1,000. Treat small corporations with assets less than $500,000 as individual donors.

Sample corporate funding index card.

Ameripol Oil Corp.	SIC: 1311
111 Broadway	GI: .007
Oklahoma City, OK 73100	BTE:
(505) 583-7092	Est. Gift:
Crude Oil and Gas Producer	
Employees: 1500	

NAME	POSITION
Victor R. Schultz	Ch Bd
William O. McCoombe	Pr.
Oscar M. Stevensen	Exec. VP
D. Samuel Kruze	Tr + Comp

GENEROSITY INDEX

The generosity index is a measure of a company's charitable giving. The higher the index, the more generous the company. The GI is the percent of before-tax earnings donated annually. Notice banks are the most generous, giving 2.09 percent annually. Use the Standard Industrial Classification (SIC) number to identify industries.

Industry Type	*SIC Number*	*GI*[a]
AGRICULTURE, FORESTRY, AND FISHERY	0111-0971	.0060
MINING	1011-1499	.0019
Metals	1011-1099	.0044
Coal	1111-1213	.0070
Crude Petroleum and Natural Gas	1311-1389	.0007
Nonmetallic (except fuels)	1411-1499	.0142
CONTRACT CONSTRUCTION	1521-1799	.0100
MANUFACTURING	2011-3999	.0098
Food and Kindred Products	2011-2099	.0106
Tobacco Manufacturers	2111-2141	.0058
Textile Mill Products	2211-2299	.0144
Apparel and Other Fabricated Textile Products	2311-2399	.0153
Lumber and Wood Products (except Furniture)	2411-2499	.0093
Furniture and Fixtures	2511-2599	.0109
Paper and Allied Products	2611-2661	.0142
Printing and Publishing	2711-2795	.0163
Chemicals and Allied Products	2812-2899	.0095
Petroleum Refining and Related Industries	2911-2999	.0049
Rubber and Miscellaneous Plastic Products	3011-3079	.0083
Leather and Leather Products	3111-3199	.0184
Stone, Clay and Glass Products	3211-3299	.0087
Primary Metal Industries	3312-3399	.0146
Fabricated Metal Products (except Machinery and Transportation Equipment)	3411-3499	.0092
Machinery (except Electrical)	3511-3599	.0092
Electrical Equipment and Supplies	3612-3699	.0101
Motor Vehicles and Equipment	3711-3715	.0093
Transportation Equipment (except Motor Vehicles)	3721-3799	.0115
Scientific Instruments, Photographic Equipment, Watches, and Clocks	3811-3873	.0079
Miscellaneous Manufactured Products and Manufacturing Not Allocable	3911-3999	.0102
TRANSPORTATION, COMMUNICATION, ELECTRIC, GAS, AND SANITARY SERVICES	4011-4971	.0093
Transportation	4011-4789	.0096
Communication	4811-4899	.0083
Electric, Gas and Sanitary Services	4911-4971	.0099
WHOLESALE AND RETAIL TRADE	5012-5999	.0093
Wholesale	5012-5199	.0079
Machinery, Equipment, and Supplies	5012-5139	.0054
Groceries and Related Products	5141-5149	.0104
Miscellaneous Wholesale	5152-5199	.0082
Retail	5211-5999	.0106
Building Materials, Hardware, and Farm Equipment	5211-5271	.0090

General Merchandise	5311-5399	.0149
Food Stores	5411-5499	.0088
Automotive Dealers and Service Stations	5511-5599	.0093
Apparel and Accessory Stores	5611-5699	.0106
Furniture, Home Furnishings, and Equipment Stores	5712-5733	.0114
Eating and Drinking Places	5812-5813	.0054
Miscellaneous Retail Stores	5912-5995	.0080
Wholesale and Retail Trade Not Allocable	5999	.0130
FINANCE, INSURANCE, REAL ESTATE	6011-6799	.0076
Banking	6011-6059	.0209
Credit Agencies Other Than Banks	6112-6163	.0106
Security and Commodity Brokers, Dealers, Exchanges, and Services	6211-6281	.0099
Insurance Carriers	6311-6399	.0050
Insurance Agents, Brokers, and Service	6411	.0105
Real Estate	6512-6553	.0069
Holding and Other Investment Companies	6711-6799	.0014
SERVICES	7011-8999	.0085
Hotels and Other Lodging Places	7011-7041	.0084
Personal Services	7211-7299	.0106
Business Services	7311-7399	.0074
Automobile Services and Miscellaneous Repair Services	7512-7699	.0060
Amusement and Recreation Services	7911-7999	.0112
Other Services	8011-8999	.0083
NATURE OF BUSINESS NOT ALLOCABLE		.0064
Average all industry		.0100

[a]To change to percent move decimal two places to the right.

PRIORITIZING POTENTIAL CORPORATE DONORS

Which Corporations Do You Approach First?

Questions to Ask

☐ Is the corporation local?

☐ What is the maximum you can expect the corporation to give?

☐ Do you, or any of your board members, know any of the corporation's executives?

☐ What is the corporation's past giving record?

☐ Do your needs match the corporate needs?

☐ Has this year been a profitable one for the corporation?

☐ Does the corporation need an improved public image?

NOTE: The corporation with the most positive answers is the best prospect and should be approached first.

CORPORATE CULTIVATION FORM

Name of Corporation _____

Address _____ Alternate Location _____

_____   _____

Phone _____ Phone _____

Nature of Business _____

Decision Maker _____ Contact Person _____

Title _____ Nickname _____

Position _____

Positions on other boards _____

Personal Data

Spouse _____ Children _____

Spouse's Occupation _____ Children's Occupation _____

Community Interests _____

Hobbies _____

Religion _____ Church Affiliation, if any _____

Political Advisors _____

Legal Advisors _____

Financial Advisors _____

Past Giving Record _____

Net Worth _____

Area(s) of Interest _____

Geographic Region(s) Funded _____

Other:

_____

Cultivation Record

Researcher _____ Date _____

THE INITIAL PHONE CALL

For Small Foundations
or Corporations

1. _____ Plan or rehearse your phone call (purpose of the phone call is to get you into a meeting with the chief decision maker).
2. _____ State your name, title, and organization.
3. _____ Show you have done your research.
"I see that your foundation/corporation has been/is involved in programs for...."
4. _____ Give reason for your call.
"We are planning a...."
"Do you have a few minutes to talk?"
If no, "When can I call back?"
5. _____ In 250 words or less, paint the benefits of your project (both for the community and for the corporation).
6. _____ Ask the funding source if they might be interested in supporting a project which provided these benefits.
If yes, set up a meeting and end the conversation immediately.
If no, find out why and determine more about the funding source and obtain at least one referral.

THE LETTER PROPOSAL

Keep the proposal short and in letter form (under six pages including attachments).

Elements of the Proposal
☐ Introductory statement
☐ Objectives of your proposal
☐ Description of your program and its operations
☐ What your program will do for the community
☐ Particular relevance to the corporation
☐ Budget: salaries, materials, services
☐ Attachments: brochure, news clippings, 501(c)(3) letter, and possibly a recent auditor's report

detroit producers association

President
SHARON BURKE
Independent

Immed. Past President
DAN NISSLY
General Television Network

First Vice-President
LEON CHICK
Producers Color Service

Second Vice-President
JACK WERTZ
New Detroit, Inc.

Secretary
NANCY KELLEY
Station 12

Treasurer
BILL SMITH
Allied Film Lab.

Directors:

BOB BURRELL
Victor Duncan, Inc.

HAFORD KERBAWY
Kerbawy & Co.

DICK REIHM
Reihm A/V

DICK SALAY
Salay/Miles Prod.

HAL YOUNGBLOOD
WJR

Admin. Comm. Chairman
ED LAMB
Ed Lamb - YMD

Active Comm. Member
DAVE GIBBONS
Gibbons & Clark

January 11, 1980

Ms. Lee Duncan, Vice President
Victor Duncan Inc.
32380 Howard Street
Madison Heights, Michigan

Dear Ms. Duncan:

The Detroit Producers Association recently described to you its plans to hold a film and television production seminar-workshop. This letter is to serve as a formal proposal to your corporation asking for its cooperation and help in its financial support.

At present, an alarming two million dollars of film and television production in the commercial-industrial film categories is being produced outside the state of Michigan. Local advertisers who wish to take advantage of innovative techniques and equipment in media production must take their business to New York, or Hollywood. These two areas have been acclaimed the major feature length film and national commercial advertising centers in the United States. As you are well aware, this is a major concern for Michigan producers, technicians and production facilities.

The Detroit Producers Association, in conjunction with the Michigan Office of Film and Television Services, has come up with the Michigan Film and Television Workshop, a cooperative venture that will help to alleviate this problem. As demonstrated by the success of the 1978 and 1979 DPA media seminars, this type of activity is one of the best methods available for conveying information on new nationally used techniques, methods, and equipment to a local media industry.

The objectives of this seminar are as follows:

(1) To enlighten the Michigan media industry of new and innovative techniques and methods in film and tape production.

(2) To develop a greater economic impact by retaining Michigan production dollars presently being spent outside the state.

635 W. Goldengate, Detroit, MI 48235 • (313) 642-7703

48   Sample letter proposal.

Ms. Lee Duncan
January 11, 1980
Page Two

The seminar will be jointly coordinated between the Detroit Producers Association and the Michigan Office of Film and Television Services, and will take place at the General Television Network facilities from September 22 through September 26. The seminar will utilize existing resources and facilities such as sound studios, laboratories, and editing facilities.

The seminar will offer instruction on the following topics:

       (1)   Motion Picture Direction
       (2)   Cimematography
       (3)   Sound Recording
       (4)   Motion Picture Editing
       (5)   Video Direction
       (6)   Video Camera Operation
       (7)   Special Effects
       (8)   Lighting
       (9)   Sound Editing

The seminar will benefit the city and state as far as (1) dollars spent during the duration of the event; (2) national exposure in the trades; (3) proving Detroit capable of holding such an event; and (4) increased growth in the industry with the creation of more jobs and more contracts for existing businesses.

Our proposal, therefore, hastens to meet the needs of the Michigan media industry.

The total cost of the project will be $75,000. Your generous contribution will not only benefit your own corporation and technicians, but will benefit the entire Michigan film and television industry as a whole. A seminar of this magnitude will bring national recognition to Detroit and enhance its image as a technically capable media production center.

If there are any further questions, please do not hesitate to contact me personally.

Sincerely,

Jack Wertz

Jack Wertz
Project Coordinator

Sample listings from mailing list catalog.

49

Sample acknowledgment device.

20 Largest Company-Sponsored Foundations

Ford Motor Company Fund
Atlantic Richfield Foundation
Alcoa Foundation
United States Steel Foundation, Inc.
Xerox Fund
Exxon Education Foundation
Procter & Gamble Fund
Mobil Foundation, Inc.
Minnesota Mining and Manufacturing Foundation, Inc.
Gulf Oil Foundation of Delaware
Eastman Kodak Charitable Trust
Amoco Foundation, Inc.
Dayton Hudson Foundation
Monsanto Fund
General Motors Foundation
General Electric Foundation
General Mills Foundation
Exxon USA Foundation
Shell Companies Foundation, Incorporated
BankAmerica Foundation

Source: *Foundation Directory*, 7th Ed. (New York: The Foundation Center, 1979).

FUNDING STRATEGY PORTFOLIO

EXERCISE 1
Identify twenty to twenty-five corporations within the twenty-five mile area appropriate to your project to which you would make a personal solicitation. Enclose data on each corporation, including earnings, estimated gifts, number of employees, location, executive officers, contact person, and other pertinent information. Information should be presented on index cards.

EXERCISE 2
Criticize the same letter proposal found in this chapter, paying particular attention to the seven elements of a good corporate proposal.

EXERCISE 3

Develop a brief letter proposal with attachments suitable for presentation to the corporation. Develop an outline of topics to be discussed with the corporate official. Describe the initial contact and who from your organization would make it.

BIBLIOGRAPHY

BROWNRIGG, W. GRANT. *Corporate Fund-Raising: A Practical Plan of Action.* American Council for the Arts, 570 7th Avenue, New York, N.Y. 10018, 1978.

Complete Grants Sourcebook for Higher Education. American Council on Education, One Dupont Circle, Washington, D.C. 20036, 1980.

Corporate 500: The Directory of Corporate Philanthropy. Gale Research Company, Book Tower, Detroit, Mich. 48226. Lists contributions of the nation's 500 largest corporations.

Corporate Foundation Directory. Taft Products, Inc., 1000 Vermont Avenue, Washington, D.C. 20005, 1979. Basic information about over 250 corporate foundations.

Corporate Foundation Profiles. The Foundation Center, 888 7th Avenue, 1980.

Corporate Fund Raising Directory. Public Service Materials Center, 355 Lexington Avenue, New York, N.Y. 10017, 1980.

Dun & Bradstreet Million Dollar Directory, Vols. I, II, and III. Dun's Marketing Services, Three Century Drive, Parsippany, N.J. 07094. Annual publication. Volume I lists 50,000 companies with assets of $1 million or more; Volume II lists companies with assets in the $500,000 to $1 million range; and Volume III lists small privately held companies. Each volume has a complete index and is arranged alphabetically and by geographic location. Each gives the name of the company, address, phone number, line of business, the SIC number, number of employees, sales volume, financial strength, officers, and board members.

Dun & Bradstreet Reference Book of Manufacturers. Dun & Bradstreet, 99 Church St., New York, N.Y. 10007.

Dun & Bradstreet's Directory of Corporate Managements. Dun's Marketing Services, Three Century Drive, Parsippany, N.J. 07094. Annual publication.

Forbes Market 500. New York: Forbes. Published in May.

Fortune Double 500 Directory. Trenton, N.J.: Fortune. Published annually.

HILLMAN, HOWARD. *The Art of Winning Corporate Grants*. New York: Vanguard Press, 1980.

How to Find Information About Companies. Washington Researchers, 910 17th Street, N.W., Washington, D.C. 20006, 1979.

KOCH, FRANK. *The New Corporate Philanthropy: How Society and Business Can Profit*. New York: Plenum Publishing Corporation, 1979.

Moody's Bank and Finance Directory. Moody's Investors Service, Inc., 99 Church Street, New York, N.Y. 10007.

Moody's Handbook of Common Stocks. Moody's Investors Service, Inc., 99 Church Street, New York, N.Y. 10007. Gives basic financial and business information on over 900 stocks.

Moody's Industrial Directory. Moody's Investors Service, Inc., 99 Church Street, New York, N.Y. 10007.

Moody's Public Utility Directory. Moody's Investors Service, Inc., 99 Church Street, New York, N.Y. 10007.

National Directory of Arts Support by Business Corporations. Washington International Arts Letter, Box 9005, Washington, D.C. 20003, 1979.

PORTER, ROBERT A. *Guide to Corporate Giving in the Arts 2*. Council for the Arts, 570 Seventh Ave., New York, N.Y. 10018.

Profiles of Involvement: The Handbook of Corporate Social Responsibility. Human Resources Network, 2010 Chancellor Street, Philadelphia, PA 19103, 1976.

Standard & Poor's Register of Corporations, Directors and Executives. 345 Hudson Street, New York, N.Y. 10014. Three volumes. Volume I is comparable to the *Million Dollar Directory*, Vol. I.

Standard & Poor's Standard Stock Reports. 345 Hudson Street, New York, N.Y. 10014. Covers 3,750 stocks and security issues drawn from the New York Stock Exchange, the American Exchange, and over-the-counter and regional exchanges. Gives total income, net income before taxes, before-tax earnings (BTE), and SIC number.

WAGNER, SUSAN E. *A Guide to Corporate Giving in the Arts*. American Council for the Arts, 570 7th Avenue, New York, N.Y. 10018, 1979.

QUIZ

Answer true or false.

1. Corporate philanthropy is based upon *quid pro quo*.
2. *The Million Dollar Directory* lists corporations with assets of $1 million to $5 million only.

3. The IRS allows corporations to give 5 percent of their before-tax earnings to charitable organizations.

4. Banks are the most generous of all corporations.

5. Personal contact with a corporation is probably the best source to obtain that company's giving record.

6. *Moody's Corporate Directory* provides a ready listing of companies which donate regularly to charitable organizations.

7. Corporations give away money to nonprofit organizations mainly because of the tax advantage.

8. Your best source of corporate giving is your own board of directors.

9. The corporate proposal should be the first contact in fund raising efforts.

10. Corporate giving has historically been 5 percent of before-tax earnings.

Answers: (1) T, (2) F, (3) T, (4) T, (5) T, (6) F, (7) F, (8) F, (9) T, (10) F.

Chapter 4

INDIVIDUAL GIVING

Giving has always been a natural tendency among human beings. Thus the saying, "people give to people," will never be more relevant than in the area of individual giving. Individuals give nine out of every ten philanthropic dollars. They give cash, material goods, and property during their lifetime and make bequests and set up trusts upon their demise. They tend to give to causes in their own city.

People give only to those they know and trust. Wealthy people give to wealthy people. Thus, you must either be wealthy or include at least one wealthy individual on your board. Ideally your board then becomes your entree into the individual giving arena. Wealthy people give to organizations they trust. Thus, you must establish the kind of reputation that hospitals, universities, and museums enjoy.

Every organization should have an individual giving program as a part of its diversified funding strategy. To build yours, you should expect to spend countless hours in the library searching through society columns and *Who's Who*. You must also be prepared to attend as many events in town as possible in order to get to know those individuals who give. They in turn get to know you and become familiar with your organization. You will develop invaluable in-house information on potential donors. In the fund raising process, you will also need to classify individuals according to their giving capability. Your board members can be helpful in identifying, classifying, and cultivating potential donors. Remember that the successful fund raiser is able to match the organization's interests to the donor's interests. Asking for the gift closes the fund raising process.

You must have a flawless accounting system and remember to properly acknowledge all gifts. Some major donors will prefer to remain anonymous.

$1 million donated

The Performing Arts Center is $1 million closer this week.

Leslie Scott, vice president for development, announced to trustees Friday that he had received $1 million for the center from someone "who prefers to remain anonymous."

The 100 plus spectators greeted the announcement with much applause.

This chapter will help you develop your individual giving program. It provides techniques for approaching major donors ($100 gift or more). You will learn how to set up a fund raising pyramid and how to identify and classify donors according to their giving capabilities. Public and semipublic sources of information are included along with a sample prospect card for compiling and storing information. As your system grows, you will want to investigate the possibility of computer-assisted storage for your individual giving campaign. This chapter also includes guidelines for using a professional fund raiser and standards for professional philanthropy. Don't forget to include restaurants, drug stores, hardware stores, clothing and other retail stores, service stations, hairdressers, and small firms as individual givers.

THE FUNDING PYRAMID

For a Million-Dollar Campaign

PYRAMID INSTRUCTIONS
There must be one gift at the top which represents 10 percent of the total amount to be raised.

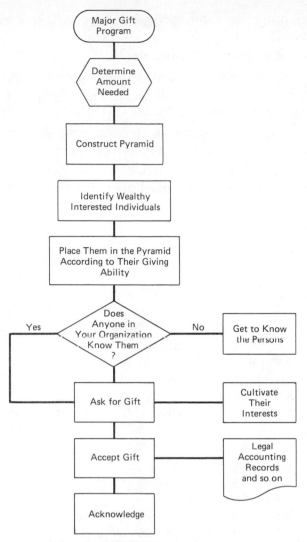

Individual giving flow chart.

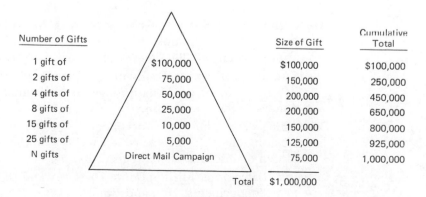

Number of Gifts		Size of Gift	Cumulative Total
1 gift of	$100,000	$100,000	$100,000
2 gifts of	75,000	150,000	250,000
4 gifts of	50,000	200,000	450,000
8 gifts of	25,000	200,000	650,000
15 gifts of	10,000	150,000	800,000
25 gifts of	5,000	125,000	925,000
N gifts	Direct Mail Campaign	75,000	1,000,000
	Total	$1,000,000	

You must have ten prospects per gift at every level of the pyramid.

Start at the top and work down.

You must place the wealthy donor at the proper level.

Your board members can assist with the task of placing persons at the correct level.

If you cannot determine the giving history of an individual, generally 5 percent of net income is a rule of thumb to ask for.

The pyramid must be realistic. That is, you must be able to fill in the pyramid with potential givers or you must redetermine the total amount needed.

PUBLIC SOURCES OF INFORMATION

Direct Mail List Rates and Data. Published by Standard Rate and Data Service, Inc., 6201 Old Orchard Rd., Skokie, Ill. 60077.

The New York Times Biographical Service. Arno Press, Inc., 3 Park Avenue, New York, N.Y. 10016. A monthly compilation of biographical information of general interest.

Who's Who In America. Marquis Who's Who, Inc., 200 East Ohio Street, Chicago, Ill. 60611. Two volumes updated yearly, with over 70,000 entries. This is a standard reference book, and almost every library has a copy. Other directories by Marquis are

> *Who's Who in the West*
> *Who's Who in the Midwest*
> *Who's Who in the East*
> *Who's Who in the South and Southwest*
> *Who's Who in Finance and Industry*
> *Who's Who in American Politics*
> *Who's Who in Art*

Who's Who Among Black Americans. Who's Who Among Black Americans, Inc. Northbrook, Ill. Gives biographical information on approximately 10,000 noteworthy black Americans.

The Foundation Directory, Foundation Center. Provides an alphabetical listing of officers and board members of foundations. It also lists donors to the foundation.

Social Registers: The New York Social Register or *Social Lists of Washington, D.C.* Check your locality for the availability of a formal or informal social register listing.

Corporate Directories: Million Dollar Directory and *Directory of Corporate Managements,* Dun and Bradstreet.

Various other sources of public information are newspapers, journals, *Polk's City Directory*, Yellow Pages, alumni lists, membership lists, books published, plaques in public places, information librarians, and media persons.

SEMIPUBLIC SOURCES OF INFORMATION

Social registers (published and unpublished).

Membership lists (country clubs, fraternities and sororities, alumni, religious organizations, civic associations, and society memberships).

Stationery from other organizations.

Plaques on walls.

Who knows whom, plays golf with, socializes with, and so on.

References from those who have already given:

The obscure or anonymous giver. Your job is to find them and match your interests to theirs. The butcher, hairdresser, banker, minister can help you to identify the obscure potential giver and their interests.

Your own in-house donor file.

Sample prospect card: the back of the card is used to record giving history.

NAME AND HOME ADDRESS	GRAD.	PREFERRED NAME	DATE OF BIRTH					
	CLASS YEAR	MARITAL STATUS	S	M	W	X	D	?
	DEGREE	INDIVIDUAL INCOME	FAMILY INCOME					
NAME OF HUSBAND OR WIFE (MAIDEN)	CLASS YEAR	ACTIVITY INTEREST						
PRESENT EMPLOYER								
BUSINESS ADDRESS - STREET		CURRENT ORGANIZATIONS, MEMBERSHIP						
CITY STATE ZIP CODE								
TITLE OR POSITION		ADDITIONAL COMMENTS						
TYPE OF BUSINESS								
PHONE BUSINESS HOME								
BUSINESS DATA								

STANDARDS FOR PHILANTHROPY

Philanthropy is considered big business in this country. Over $40 billion are entrusted annually to philanthropic organizations. To insure the ideals of philanthropic giving, several organizations have developed standards which should be followed when soliciting contributions nationally from the general public. The National Information Bureau, Inc., has published the following list of basic standards in philanthropy:*

1. *Board*—An active and responsible governing body, holding regular meetings, whose members have no material conflict of interest and serve without compensation.
2. *Purpose*—A clear statement of purpose in the public interest.
3. *Program*—A program consistent with the organization's stated purpose and its personnel and financial resources, and involving interagency cooperation to avoid duplication of work.
4. *Expenses*—Reasonable program, management, and fund raising expenses.
5. *Promotion*—Ethical publicity and promotion excluding exaggerated or misleading claims.
6. *Fund raising*—Solicitation of contribution without payment of commissions or undue pressure, such as mailing unordered tickets of merchandise, general telephone solicitation, and use of identified government employees as solicitors.

7. *Accountability*—An annual report available on request that describes program activities and supporting services in relation to expenses, and includes detailed financial statements employing Uniform Accounting Standards, accompanied by a report of an independent public accountant.
8. *Budget*—Detailed annual budget approved by the governing body in a form consistent with annual financial statements.

USING A PROFESSIONAL FUND RAISER

The professional fund raiser is most useful when your capital fund raising campaign approaches a goal of over $1 million. There are two reasons why you should consider hiring the

Wise Giving for Contributors (New York: National Information Bureau, Inc., 1979).

services of a professional fund raising firm rather than running this type of campaign on your own. The first is that the professional firms have qualified, experienced staff who can develop the materials and organize the workers for a major fund raising effort. The second is that the professional fund raiser can identify individuals and corporations who are, so to speak, beyond your reach.

The credible professional fund raising firm will provide a free initial inquiry, and then set a fixed fee for the feasibility study and another fee for the actual campaign. Do not do business with a firm that operates on a contingency percentage or commission basis. This places undo pressure on potential donors and is considered unethical by credible philanthropic organizations.

The services of the professional fund raising firms are expensive, and often beyond the budget capacity of many organizations. However, you can get relatively inexpensive advice from the professionals by attending their workshops and following their literature.

To guide you in your interaction with professional fund raisers the American Association of Fund-Raising Counsel, Inc., has published the following "Fair Practice Code":*

Members of the Association are firms which are exclusively or primarily organized to provide fund-raising counseling services, feasibility studies, campaign management and related public relations, to nonprofit institutions and agencies seeking philanthropic support. They will not knowingly be used by an organization to induce philanthropically inclined persons to give their money to unworthy causes.

Member firms do business only on the basis of a fixed fee. They will not serve clients on the unprofessional basis of a contingency, or of a percentage or commission of the sums raised. Intended services and fees are defined in contractual relationships, and additional services, as required, are furnished by mutual agreement. Member firms may not offer or provide the services of professional solicitors.

The executive head of a member organization must demonstrate at least a six-year record of continuous experience as a professional in the fund-raising field. This helps to protect the public

---

Giving USA: 1980 Annual Report (New York: American Association of Fund-Raising Counsel, Inc., 1980).

from those who enter the profession without sufficient compe-tence, experience, or devotion to ideals of public service.

The Association looks with disfavor upon firms which use methods harmful to the public, such as making exaggerated claims of past achievements, guaranteeing results, and promis-ing to raise unobtainable sums.

No payment in cash or kind shall be made by a member to an officer, director, trustee, or advisor of a philanthropic agency or institution as compensation for using his influence for the engaging of a member for fund-raising counsel.

In fairness to all clients, member firms should charge equitable fees for all services with the exception that initial meetings with prospective clients are not usually construed as services.

For more advice and information on using professional fund raisers in your funding strategy you should contact one of the national organizations related to philanthropy.

NATIONAL ORGANIZATIONS
RELATED TO PHILANTHROPY

American Association of Fund-Raising Counsel, Inc., 500 Fifth Avenue, New York, N.Y. 10036.

American Association of Museums, 2223 Wisconsin Avenue, N.W., Washington, D.C. 20007.

American Council for the Arts, (formerly Associated Councils for the Arts), 570 Seventh Avenue, New York, N.Y. 10018.

American Council on Education, One Dupont Circle, Washington, D.C. 20036.

American Hospital Association, 840 North Lake Shore Drive, Chicago, Ill. 60611.

American Symphony Orchestra League, P.O. Box 66, Vienna, Va. 22180.

Association of American Colleges, 1818 R Street, N.W., Washington, D.C. 20009.

Business Committee for the Arts, Inc., 1700 Broadway, New York, N.Y. 10019.

Coalition of National Voluntary Organizations, 1828 L Street, N.W., Washington, D.C. 20036.

Committee for Economic Development, 477 Madison Avenue, New York, N.Y. 10022.

The Conference Board, 845 Third Avenue, New York, N.Y. 10022.

Council for Advancement and Support of Education, One Dupont Circle, Washington, D.C. 20036.

Council for Financial Aid to Education, Inc., 680 Fifth Avenue, New York, N.Y. 10019.

Council of Better Business Bureaus, Inc., 1150 17th Street, N.W., Washington, D.C. 20036.

Council of Jewish Federations, 575 Lexington Avenue, New York, N.Y. 10036.

Council of State Governments, 36 West 44th Street, New York, N.Y. 10036.

Council on Foundations, Inc., 1828 L Street, N.W., Washington, D.C. 20036.

Federation of Protestant Welfare Agencies, 251 Fourth Avenue, New York, N.Y. 10010.

Foundation Center, 888 Seventh Avenue, New York, N.Y. 10106.

Independent College Funds of America, Inc., 5108 Empire State Building, New York, N.Y. 10001.

Lutheran Resources Commission-Washington, 1346 Connecticut Avenue, N.W., Washington, D.C. 20036.

National Assembly of National Voluntary Health and Social Welfare Organization, Inc., 291 Broadway, New York, N.Y. 10017.

National Association for Hospital Development, 1700 K Street, N.W., Washington, D.C. 20036.

National Association of Independent Colleges and Universities, 1717 Massachusetts Avenue, Washington, D.C. 20036.

National Association of Independent Schools, Inc., 4 Liberty Square, Boston, Mass. 02184.

National Catholic Development Conference, 119 North Park Avenue, Rockville Centre, N.Y. 11570.

National Catholic Education Association, One Dupont Circle, Washington, D.C. 20036.

National Catholic Stewardship Council, 1234 Massachusetts Avenue, N.W., Washington, D.C. 20005.

National Catholic Welfare Conference, 1312 Massachusetts Avenue, N.W., Washington, D.C. 20005.

National Center for Voluntary Action, 1214 16th Street, N.W., Washington, D.C. 20036.

National Committee for Responsive Philanthropy, 1028 Connecticut Avenue, N.W., Washington, D.C. 20036.

National Council of Churches, 475 Riverside Drive, New York, N.Y. 10027.

National Council on Philanthropy, 1828 L Street, N.W., Washington, D.C. 20036.

National Health Council, 1740 Broadway, New York, N.Y. 10019.

National Information Bureau, Inc., 419 Park Avenue South, New York, N.Y. 10016.

National Society of Fund Raising Executives, 1511 K Street, N.W., Washington, D.C. 20005.

Philanthropic Advisory Service Council of Better Business Bureaus, Inc., Washington, D.C. 20036.

Tax Foundation, 50 Rockefeller Plaza, New York, N.Y. 10020.

United Negro College Fund, 500 East 62nd Street, New York, N.Y. 10021.

United Way of America, 801 North Fairfax Street, Alexandria, Va. 22314.

FUNDING STRATEGY PORTFOLIO

EXERCISE 1

Identify a minimum of twenty-five individuals in a location appropriate to your project to be considered as potential major givers. Compile information about the giver, his or her background, interests, giving history, estimated gift, and so on. Put the information on index cards for future reference.

EXERCISE 2

Construct an individual giving funding pyramid for your project and indicate where the twenty-five individuals fit into the pyramid. (*Note:* Your actual pyramid will call for more than twenty-five individuals. This exercise is intended to get you started in your individual giving campaign.) Determine who or what type of person you will use to classify each individual's giving capability. Select those people you will use in the solicitation process.

EXERCISE 3

Briefly describe the nature of the solicitation process you will use to cultivate the prospects. This should include a schedule of whom you will approach and the order in which the contacts will be made.

BIBLIOGRAPHY

Individual Giving in General

ANDREWS, F. EMERSON. *Attitudes Toward Giving.* New York: Russell Sage Foundation, 1953.

HUTLER, ALBERT A. *Guide to Successful Fund-Raising.* Larchmont, N.Y.: Business Reports, Inc., 1977.

Income Tax Deduction for Contributions. IRS Publication 526.

SEYMOUR, HAROLD. *Designs for Fund-Raising: Principles, Patterns, Techniques.* New York: McGraw-Hill, Inc., 1966.

Valuation of Donated Properties. IRS Publication 561.

Planned Giving

If your organization is well established in the community and intends to be around for the next one hundred years, you should have a planned giving program intact.

BROSTERMAN, ROBERT. *The Complete Estate Planning Guide.* New York: Mentor Book, 1970.

Deferred Giving. Washington, D.C.: American Alumni Council, 1977.

Estate Planning in Gift Development. Newkirk Associates, Inc., Professional Education Division, 308 Wolf Road, Latham, N.Y. 12110, 1972.

FREEMAN, DOUGLAS K., "The Charitable Partner in Family Estate Planning," in *Charitable Giving and Solicitation.* Englewood Cliffs, N.J.: Prentice-Hall, Inc., 1981.

Guide to the Administration of Charitable Remainder Trusts. The Council for Advancement and Support of Education (CASE), Box 298, Alexandria, Va. 22314, 1978.

KING, GEORGE V. *Deferred Gifts: How to Get Them.* The Fund Raising Institute, 1980. Box 365, Ambler, Pa. 19002.

KUTNER, LUIS. *Legal Aspects of Charitable Trusts and Foundations.* New York: Commerce Clearing House, 1970.

SHARPE, ROBERT. *The Planned Giving Idea Book: Creative Ways to Increase the Income of Your Institution.* Thomas Nelson, Inc., 1978. 407 7th Avenue, So., Nashville, Tenn. 37203.

SHEPPARD, WILLIAM E. *Bequest Program Handbook.* The Fund Raising Institute, 1970. Box 365, Ambler, Pa. 19002.

WILLIAMS, JANE M. *Capital Ideas: Step by Step How to Solicit Major Gifts From Private Sources.* The Fund Raising Institute, Box 365, Ambler, Pa. 19002, 1979.

QUIZ

Answer true or false.

1. The greatest source of philanthropic funds is individuals.
2. Individuals, corporations, and foundations all tend to give primarily to organizations in their own locale.
3. In your $1 million individual fund raising campaign, you must identify ten persons each capable of giving a $100,000 gift at the top of your funding pyramid.
4. The single most important thing you will do in individual giving is select your first board member.
5. As a good fund raiser, you are able to match the donor's interests to your organization's interests.
6. In identifying obscure givers, friends of their children or grandchildren are often the most helpful source to start with.
7. Your board member is your number one resource in approaching major donors.
8. Bequests, memorial gifts, deferred and planned gifts are probably unrealistic gifts to ask for unless your organization plans to be in operation for one hundred years.
9. There are virtually no laws in this country regarding the public solicitation of charitable funds.
10. Anonymous gifts are not allowed in charitable giving.

Answers: (1) T, (2) T, (3) T, (4) T, (5) T, (6) F, (7) T, (8) T, (9) T, (10) F.

Chapter 5

INDIVIDUAL GIVING
BY DIRECT MAIL

Direct mail accounts for over one-third of the philanthropic giving in this country. Every organization should have a direct mail campaign as a part of its funding strategy.

Every organization has a membership, and direct mail can be a means of tapping that membership for dollars and volunteers. Direct mail is probably the most technically complex method of obtaining funds for your organization, and because it requires a sizeable capital investment, it is often not considered. On the other hand, individual giving by direct mail is aimed at the smaller gift and as such can be an invaluable source of operating funds for your organization. It is also a way to begin to identify and cultivate major givers. Many small nonprofit organizations are capable of organizing a yearly direct mail campaign using volunteer labor, in-town contributions of artwork, donated printing, and the like.

This chapter is designed to help small organizations get started on their own and help other organizations who contract for services be familiar with the basic terminology when dealing with a professional firm.

Start by mailing to your membership. Then broaden your mailing to include a select audience in the community. You will need to know how to identify and use existing lists and how to construct and maintain your own list. You will need to develop a complete direct mail package including the envelopes, letter, and enclosures. By using Addressograph, Xerox labels, or computer files, you will be better able to organize and maintain a clean house list. You must decide on a mail, return mail, and accounting procedure. Above all, you will need to test the effectiveness of your package as you proceed.

FROM PROSPECT LIST
TO HOUSE LIST

You spend $1,000 on a direct mail campaign and get $1,000 in return. Has it been worth it?

A *prospect list* contains the names and addresses of potential givers based on demographic or special interests. It is used for an initial mailing with the intent of building a house list.

A *house list* contains those individuals who have responded positively to your organization, usually through the initial mailing.

The rules of individual giving by direct mail apply primarily to the prospect list and the initial mailing. Your task is to build as large a house list as possible.

As a rule, it matters less what you mail if you mail it to the "right" person.

Incidentally the answer to the question above is yes, if this is your first campaign. You have gotten publicity and you now have a house list of people who have contributed to your program. Note, however, that breaking even is a sign that there are some flaws in your direct mail program.

MAILING LISTS

Types of Lists

Demographic-Based Lists in Increasing Order of Priority
occupant
telephone
city directory

credit card holders (American Express, Diners Club, Carte Blanche)

mail order catalog buyers

Special Interest Lists
occupational lists

magazine and journal subscribers

Donors Lists
These lists are most effective because they contain people who contribute regularly.

How to Obtain Lists

The Direct Mail List Rates and Data Catalog contains several thousand lists, where they can be obtained, cost, list certification, and other pertinent information.

Some Major Mailing List Companies

R. L. Polk

Dunhill International

R. H. Donnelly

Dun and Bradstreet

The Mechanics of Renting a List

Your best bet is to deal with a list broker rather than a list owner because the list selection will be greater. Rent the list and remember that the list will be "salted" with phoney mail addresses so you must get approval each time you use it. Note that responses from the list go on your house list and are yours to use as you wish.

Building Your Own Prospect List

Ask every staff member, board member and volunteer to supply ten to fifty names and you will have a small but high quality list. Every organization has a membership. What is yours? Use it as your basic list.

Do not include corporations in your direct mail list.

D

Subject — Class.

DAIRIES—see Dairy Products, 79
DAIRY & DAIRY BREEDS—Class. 700
DAIRY PRODUCTS—Class. 77
DANCING—Class. 526
DATA PROCESSING—see Automatic Data Systems, 15
DATA PROCESSING COURSES—see Education & Self-Improvement, 532
DEALERS (AIR CONDITIONING)—see Air Conditioning, Plumbing & Heating, etc., 5
DEALERS (ART)—see Art & Antiques, 506; also Arts, 13
DEALERS (GAS APPLIANCES)—see Appliances, 9
DEALERS (HEATING)—see Air Conditioning, Plumbing & Heating, etc., 5
DEALERS (PLUMBING)—see Air Conditioning, Plumbing & Heating, etc., 5
DEALERS (WASHING MACHINES)—see Appliances, 9
DECORATING—see Interior Design & Decorating, 171 also Paint, Painting & Decorating, 249
DECORATOR FABRICS—see Home & Family Service, 558
DECORATORS—see Home Furnishings, 147; also Interior Design & Decorating, 171; also Paint, Painting & Decorating, 249
DEFENSE CONTRACTORS—see Government Administrative Services and Public Works, 139
DELICATESSENS—see Restaurants and Food Service, 295
DEMOCRATS—see Political & Social Topics, 592
DENOMINATIONS, RELIGIOUS— see Religious, 289; also Religious & Denominational, 596
DENTAL—Class. 79
DENTAL LABORATORIES—see Dental, 79; also Medical & Surgical, 205
DENTAL PRODUCTS—see Health, 556
DENTAL SUPPLIES—see Dental, 79
DENTISTS—see Dental, 79; also Medical & Surgical, 205
DEPARTMENT, GENERAL MERCHANDISE & SPECIALTY STORES—Class. 81
DEPARTMENT STORE BUYERS (GENERAL)—see Department, General Merchandise & Specialty Stores, 81
DEPARTMENT STORE CHAINS—see Chain Stores, 53
DEPARTMENT STORE EXECUTIVES (GENERAL)—see Department, General Merchandise & Specialty Stores, 81
DEPARTMENT STORES—see Department, General Merchandise & Specialty Stores, 81, also General, 552
DESIGN ENGINEERING—see Product Design Engineering, 279
DESIGNERS, PACKAGING—see Packaging & Users, 247
DESIGNS, HOME—see Home & Family Service, 558
DETECTIVE AGENCIES—see Police, Detective & Sheriff, 267
DIARY BUYERS—see General, 552
DICTATION TRANSCRIPTION EQUIPMENT—see Office Equipment & Stationery, 235
DICTIONARIES—see Almanacs & Directories, 502
DIET—see Health, 556

Subject — Class.

DIPLOMATS, U. S.—see Government Administrative Services and Public Works, 139
DIRECT MAIL LIST BUYERS—see Advertising and Marketing, 3
DIRECT MAIL RESPONSE—refer to specific product, subject or service
DIRECT MAIL RESPONSE, GENERAL—see General Merchandise Mail Order Buyers, 553
DIRECTORIES—see Almanacs & Directories, 502
DIRECTORS, CORPORATION—see Business Executives, 45; also Business Leaders, 518
DISCIPLES OF CHRIST (CHURCHES & CLERGY)—see Religious, 289
DISC JOCKEYS—see Music & Record Buyers, 578; also Music & Music Trades, 223
DISCOUNT MARKETING—Class. 83
DISCOUNT STORES—see Discount Marketing, 83; also Department, General Merchandise & Specialty Stores, 81
DISHES—see Collectibles, 520A
DISPLAY—Class. 85
DISTILLERS—see Brewing, Distilling & Beverages, 35
DISTRIBUTION—see Co-Op Mailings, Package Insert Programs & Private Delivery Systems
DISTRIBUTORS (INDUSTRIAL)—see Industrial Distribution, 161
DISTRICT ATTORNEYS—see Legal, 185
DIVERSIFIED FARMING & FARM HOME—Class. 702
DIVORCE—see Home & Family Service, 558
DOCTORS—see Dental, 79; also Medical & Surgical, 205; also Professional, 594; also Science, Research & Development, 311
DOG GROOMERS—see Dogs & Pets, 528
DOGS & PETS—Class. 528
DO-IT-YOURSELF—see Automotive, 508; also Crafts, Hobbies & Models, 524; also Mechanics & Science, 566
DOLL FASHIONS—see Dressmaking & Needlework, 530
DONORS—see Contributors, 522; also Political & Social Topics, 592; also Religious & Denominational, 596
DRAPERIES & CURTAINS—Class. 87
DRESSES—see Fashions, 544
DRESSMAKING—see Crafts, Hobbies, Models, 524; also Dressmaking & Needlework, 530
DRESSMAKING & NEEDLEWORK—Class. 530
DRILLING CONTRACTORS—see Petroleum & Oil, 255
DRILLING (PRODUCTION)—see Petroleum & Oil, 255
DRINKING PLACES—see Brewing, Distilling & Beverage, 35
DRIVE-IN MOVIES—see Amusements, 7
DRIVE-INS (FOOD)—see Restaurants & Food Service, 295; also Food—Processing and Distribution, 121
DRUGGISTS—see Drugs, Pharmaceutics, 89
DRUGS, PHARMACEUTICS—Class. 89
DRUG STORE CHAINS—see Chain Stores, 53
DRUG STORES—see Drugs, Pharmaceutics, 89
DRUG WHOLESALERS—see Drugs, Pharmaceutics, 89
DRY CLEANING PLANTS—see Laundry & Dry Cleaning, 181
DUDE RANCHES—see Hotels, Motels, Clubs & Resorts, 151
DUPLICATING EQUIPMENT—see Office Equipment & Stationery, 235
DYEING PLANTS—see Laundry & Dry Cleaning, 181

E

ECOLOGISTS—see Pollution Control, 269; also Science, Research & Development, 311
ECONOMISTS—see Banking & Financial, 23; also Business Executives, 45
EDITORS—see Books & Book Trade, 31; also Journalism, 177
EDUCATION—see Education & Self-Improvement, 532; also Children's, 520
EDUCATIONAL—Class. 91
EDUCATION & SELF-IMPROVEMENT—Class. 532
EDUCATORS—see Educational, 91; also Schools and School Administration, 309; also Education & Self-Improvement, 532
ELECTRICAL—Class. 93
ELECTRICAL CONTRACTORS—see Electrical, 93
ELECTRIC MOTOR DEALERS—see Electrical, 93
ELECTRIC SUPPLY CHAINS—see Chain Stores, 53
ELECTRIC SUPPLY & PRODUCTION DEALERS—see Electrical, 93
ELECTRIC UTILITIES—see Electrical, 93; also Power & Power Plants, 273
ELECTRONIC ENGINEERING—Class. 95
ELECTRONIC INSTRUMENT MANUFACTURERS—see Electronic Engineering, 95
ELECTRONIC PARTS DISTRIBUTORS—see Radio & Television, 283
ELECTRONIC PURCHASING AGENTS—see Electronic Engineering, 95
ELECTRONICS—see Mechanics & Science, 566
ELECTRONIC TECHNICIANS—see Electronic Engineering, 95; also Radio & Television, 283

Subject — Class.

ELECTROPLATERS—see Chemical & Chemical Process Industries, 55
ELEMENTARY SCHOOLS—see Schools and School Administration, 309
ELEMENTARY SCHOOL TEACHERS—see Educational, 91
EMBROIDERY—see Dressmaking & Needlework, 530
EMPLOYMENT AGENCIES see Business Firms, 46
EMPLOYMENT, PART TIME—see Opportunity Seekers, 588
ENCYCLOPEDIAS— see Almanacs & Directories, 502
ENGAGEMENTS—see Brides, 516
ENGINEERING COLLEGES—see Schools and School Administration 309
ENGINEERING & CONSTRUCTION—Class. 97
ENGINEERING FIRMS see Engineers, 99
ENGINEERING SERVICES—see Business Firms, 46
ENGINEERS—Class. 99
ENGINEERS—see Engineers, 99; also Professional, 594
ENGINEERS (AIR CONDITIONING, PLUMBING & HEATING)—see Air Conditioning, Plumbing & Heating, 5
ENGINEERS (ARCHITECTURAL)—see Engineers, 99
ENGINEERS (AVIATION & AEROSPACE)—see Aviation & Aerospace, 19
ENGINEERS (CONTROL SYSTEMS)—see Control & Instrumentation Systems, 71
ENGINEERS (DEVELOPMENT)—see Business Executives, 45
ENGINEERS (ELECTRICAL & ELECTRONIC)—see Electronic Engineering, 95; also Engineering & Construction, 97; also Engineers, 99
ENGINEERS (GENERAL)—see Engineers, 99
ENGINEERS (PETROLEUM)—see Petroleum & Oil, 255
ENGINEERS, PROFESSIONAL—see Professional, 594
ENTOMOLOGISTS—see Science, Research & Development, 3'1
ENVELOPE BUYERS, OFFICE—see Office Equipment & Stationery, 235
ENVIRONMENTAL CONTROL—see Pollution Control 269; also Science, Research & Development, 311
EPICUREAN AND SPECIALTY FOODS—Class. 536
EPISCOPAL (CHURCHES & CLERGY)—see Religious, 289
EQUESTRIAN—See Horses, Riding & Breeding, 559
EQUIPMENT, LIVESTOCK—see Livestock & Breed, 716
ESTATE PLANNING—see Investors, 561
ESTATE TAXES—see General, 552
ETHNIC—Class. 538
ETIQUETTE—see Brides, 516
EVANGELICAL REFORMED (CHURCHES & CLERGY)—see Religious, 289
EXCAVATING—see Engineering & Construction, 97
EXECUTIVES (ADVERTISING)—see Business Executives, 45; also Business Leaders, 518
EXECUTIVES (AEROSPACE)—see Aviation & Aerospace, 19
EXECUTIVES (ASSOCIATION)—see Business Executives, 45
EXECUTIVES (AUTOMOTIVE JOBBERS)—see Automotive, Automobiles, Tires, etc., 17
EXECUTIVES (BUSINESS-GENERAL)—see Business Executives, 45
EXECUTIVES (CHAMBERS OF COMMERCE)—see Business Executives, 45; also Fraternal, Professional Groups, etc., 548
EXECUTIVES (CONTROL SYSTEMS)—see Control & Instrumentation Systems, 71
EXECUTIVES (GENERAL)—see Business Executives, 45
EXECUTIVES (MANUFACTURING)—see Business Firms, 46
EXECUTIVES (OFFICE)—see Business Executives, 45
EXHIBIT & TRADE SHOW FACILITIES—see Advertising & Marketing, 3
EXPECTANT MOTHERS—see Babies, 512
EXPIRATIONS, MAGAZINE—see specific product, subject or service
EXPORTING—see International Trade, 173
EXTERMINATORS—see Maintenance, 195
EXTRUDING—see Plastics & Composition Products, 263
EYEGLASSES—see Health, 556

F

FABRICATING—see Plastics & Composition Products, 263
FABRIC CLUBS—see Crafts, Hobbies & Models, 524
FABRICS—see Dressmaking & Needlework, 530
FACTORY OUTLETS—see General, 552
FAMILIES, GENERAL—see General, 552; also Home & Family Service, 558
FAMILIES, RELIGIOUS—see Religious & Denominational, 596
FAMILIES WITH CHILDREN—see Babies, 512; also Children's 520; also Home & Family Service, 558; also Teenagers, 604
FAMILIES WITH COLLEGE STUDENTS—see College and Alumni, 521
FAMILY SERVICE—see Home & Family Service, 558
FARM CO-OP MAILINGS—see Co-Op Mailings, Package Insert Programs & Private Delivery Systems.

Subject/Market Classification Index—Continued

Subject — Class.

FARM EDUCATION & VOCATIONS—Class. 704
FARMERS—see Diversified Farming & Farm Home, 702
FARMERS, LATIN AMERICAN—see Diversified Farming & Farm Home, 702
FARM IMPLEMENTS & SUPPLIES—Class. 101
FARM OPERATORS—see Diversified Farming & Farm Home, 702
FARM OWNERS—see Diversified Farming & Farm Home, 702
FARM SUPPLY STORES—see Farm Implements & Supplies, 101
FASHIONS—Class 544
FEDERAL OFFICIALS—see Government Administrative Services & Public Works, 139
FASHION ACCESSORIES—Class. 105
FEED, GRAIN AND MILLING—Class. 107
FERTILIZER—see Gardening (Home), 550
FERTILIZER & AGRICULTURAL CHEMICALS—Class. 109
FERTILIZER DUSTERS—see Fertilizer & Agricultural Chemicals, 109
FERTILIZERS—see Fertilizer & Agricultural Chemicals, 109
FICTION WRITERS—see Journalism, 177
FIELD CROPS & SOIL MANAGEMENT—Class. 710
FILM PROCESSING—see Photography, 590
FINANCE—see Investors, 561
FINANCE COMPANIES—see Banking & Financial, 23
FINANCE COMPANY CUSTOMERS—see Credit Card Holders, 525
FINANCIAL ANALYSTS—see Banking & Financial, 23
FINANCIAL BOOK BUYERS—see Banking & Financial, 23; also Investors, 561
FIRE DEPARTMENTS—see Fire Protection, 113; also Government Administrative Services & Public Works, 139
FIRE PROTECTION—Class. 113
FISHING COMMERCIAL—Class. 115
FISHING & HUNTING—Class. 546
FISHING TACKLE—see Fishing & Hunting, 546
FLATWARE—see Home & Family Service, 558
FLEET OWNERS—see Public Transportation, 281; also Motor Trucks & Accessories, 217
FLOOR COVERINGS—Class. 117
FLOOR COVERINGS—see Home & Family Service, 558
FLOORING—see Home & Family Service, 558
FLOORING & INTERIOR SERVICE DEALERS—see Floor Coverings, 117
FLORICULTURE—see Florists & Floriculture, 119
FLORISTS & FLORICULTURE—Class. 119
FLOWERS—see Gardening (Home), 550
FLOWER SHOPS—see Florists & Floriculture, 119
FOOD DISTRIBUTION—see Food Processing & Distribution, 121
FOOD ITEMS—see Epicurean, 536; also Gifts and Gift Buyers, 554

(Continued on next page)

March 2, 1979 — Direct Mail—Master Index Section — I-5

Sample listings from mailing list catalog.

Source: *Direct Mail List Rates and Data*, Consumer Lists, Standard Rate and Data Service, Inc., 5201 Old Orchard Rd., Skokie, Ill. 60077.

Source: *Direct Mail List Rates and Data*, Consumer Lists, Standard Rate and Data Service, Inc., 5201 Old Orchard Rd., Skokie, Ill. 60077.

Sample listings from mailing list catalog.

Source: *Direct Mail List Rates and Data*, Consumer Lists, Standard Rate and Data Service, Inc., 5201 Old Orchard Rd., Skokie, Ill. 60077.
Sample listings from mailing list catalog.

Affluent Society, The

Media Code 3 600 1333 8.00
Ed Burnett Consultants, Inc., 2 Park Ave., New York, N. Y. 10016. Phone 212-679-0630.
For basic information on listing segments 1, 3, 5, 7, 8, 9, 10, see Ed Burnett, Consultant listing in Mailing List Compilers section.

2. DESCRIPTION
High level business management personnel, doctors and their next door neighbors, all at home addresses. Average income 25,000.00; average value of home 80,000.00.
ZIP Coded in numerical sequence 100%.

4. QUANTITY AND RENTAL RATES
Rec'd July, 1978.

	Total Number	Price per/M
Total list	3,083,000	30.00
Affluents with incomes 25,000 plus	3,186,000	30.00
Board of directors at home addresses	65,000	30.00
Top corporate execs.	480,000	35.00
Doctors at home addresses	315,000	30.00

Selections: state, SCF, ZIP Code, sex, home owners, no charge; phone numbers 5.00/M extra; key coding 1.00/M extra.
Minimum order affluent and directors, 10,000; doctors and executives, 125.00.

6. METHOD OF ADDRESSING
4 across East-West Cheshire. Dry-vac gummed, 3.00/M extra; pressure sensitive 7.50/M extra.
Magnetic tape available (25.00 deposit).

AFFLUENT SOCIETY, THE

Media Code 3 600 1416 1.00

1. PERSONNEL
List Manager
Woodruff-Stevens & Associates, Inc., 40 E. 34th St., New York, N. Y. 10016. Phone 212-725-1555.
All recognized brokers.

2. DESCRIPTION
Combination of lists of wealthy individuals throughout the United States. Names are non-duplicated. 80% men.

4. QUANTITY AND RENTAL RATES
Rec'd January, 1979.

	Total Number	Price per/M
Total list	1,200,000	25.00
At business address	700,000	"
At home address	500,000	"

Selections: state, Nth name, 2.00/M extra; SCF, 4.00/M extra; keying (4 digits), 1.00/M extra.
Minimum order 5,000.

6. METHOD OF ADDRESSING
4-up Cheshire.
Magnetic tape available.

AFFLUENT URBAN AMERICANS

Media Code 3 600 1437 7.00
Member: D.M.M.A.
Dependable Lists, Inc., 257 Park Ave. South, New York, N. Y. 10010. Phone 212-677-6760.
For basic information on listing segments 1, 5, 6, 7, 9, 11 see Dependable Lists, Inc. listing in Classification 552.

2. DESCRIPTION
Above average persons, broken down by the 26 most important standard metropolitan areas. Annual income 25,000.00. 85% men, at home address.

3. LIST SOURCE
Directories and rosters.

4. QUANTITY AND RENTAL RATES
Rec'd September, 1978.

	Total Number	Price per/M
Total list (No. 1553/3)	790,200	27.50

Selections: state, SCF, ZIP Code, 2.50/M extra; keying, 1.00/M extra.
Minimum order 5,000.

Almost Millionaires

Media Code 3 600 1458 3.00
W. S. Ponton Inc., Of Pittsburgh, 1414 Hawthorne St., Pittsburgh, Pa. 15201. Phone 412-782-2360.
For basic information on listing segments 1, 5, 6, 7, 9, 10, 11 see W. S. Ponton Inc. of Pittsburgh listing in Classification 552.

2. DESCRIPTION
People with net worths and incomes of 750,000.00 and over.
ZIP Coded in numerical sequence 100%.
List is computerized.

3. LIST SOURCE
Directories and newspaper clippings.
Derived thru compilation 100%.

4. QUANTITY AND RENTAL RATES
Rec'd December, 1978.

	Total Number	Price per/M
Total list	90,000	48.80

State selection available.

(D-B)

CALIFORNIA BEAUTIFUL PEOPLE

Media Code 3 600 1604 2.00
Sales Promotion Services, Inc., P. O. Box 257, Tiburon, Calif. 94920. Phone 415-388-2271.

1. PERSONNEL
General Mgr./EDP—Philip J. Marcus.
Sales—Ira Cohen.
Broker and/or Authorized Agent
All recognized brokers.

2. DESCRIPTION
Merged and unduplicated names from a large number of high income and wealth lists. Includes major executive and professional lists owners of expensive homes, boats and planes, real estate, investors, etc.
ZIP Coded in numerical sequence 100%.
List is computerized.
Selections available: 5 digit ZIP Code, 3 digit ZIP Code-sectional centers.

3. LIST SOURCE
Latest directories, government files, exclusive club memberships and miscellaneous records available.
Derived thru compilation 100%.

4. QUANTITY AND RENTAL RATES
Rec'd May, 1978.

	Total Number	Price per/M
Total list	430,254	*20.00

(*) For quantities over 75,000; 2,000-4,999, 40.00/M; 5,000-19,999, 35.00/M; 20,000-49,999, 30.00/M; 50,000-74,999, 25.00/M.
Nth samples 1.00/M extra for quantities under 10,000.

5. COMMISSION, CREDIT POLICY
20% to all brokers; 15% to advertising agencies. First orders must be prepaid. Credit only to established customers.

6. METHOD OF ADDRESSING
4-up Cheshire. Pressure sensitive 6.00/M extra; magnetic tape (flat 7.50).

7. DELIVERY SCHEDULE
5 working days from P. O. is received.
48 hour rush service available 35.00 extra, or 1.50/M, whichever is greater.

8. RESTRICTIONS
Rented for one time use only. Agent or buyer assumes total responsibility for usage fee in case of reuse of list supplied.

9. TEST ARRANGEMENT
Nth samples or cross section. Split test 3.00/M extra. Minimum 3,000.

11. MAINTENANCE
Computer unduplicated and edited. Updated twice a year.

Civic Leaders in the United States At Home Address

Media Code 3 600 1677 8.00
Butler Management Corp., 0000 Sunset Blvd., Los Angeles, Calif. 90069. Phone 213-550-8000.

1. PERSONNEL
List Manager—Gene Scher.
Branch Office
New York 10022—437 Madison Ave. Phone 212-371-7333.

2. DESCRIPTION
Civic leaders in the United States at home address, compiled from 20 biographical directories and registers.

4. QUANTITY AND RENTAL RATES
Rec'd May, 1978.

	Total Number	Price per/M
Total list	303,400	30.00

Selections: state, 2.00/M extra; SCF, 4.00/M extra; key coding (4 digit maximum), 1.00/M extra.
Minimum order 5,000.

5. COMMISSION, CREDIT POLICY
20% to recognized brokers.

6. METHOD OF ADDRESSING
4 or 5-up Cheshire.
Magnetic tape available.

8. RESTRICTIONS
Sample mail piece required for approval.

CULTURE BUFFS

(This is a duplicate of the listing under Classification No. 506.)

Media Code 3 600 1750 3.00

1. PERSONNEL
List Manager
Response Mailing Lists, P. O. Box 88, North Miami Beach, Fla. 33160. Phone 305-652-1610.
All recognized brokers.

2. DESCRIPTION
Compilation of individuals interested in cultural arts.
ZIP Coded in numerical sequence 100%.

3. LIST SOURCE
Cultural Society rosters.

4. QUANTITY AND RENTAL RATES
Rec'd December, 1978.

	Total Number	Price per/M
Total list	185,000	25.00

Selections: state, 3-digit ZIP Code, Nth name, 2.50/M extra.

5. COMMISSION, CREDIT POLICY
20% to all recognized brokers, 15% to all recognized ad agencies and lettershops; all payments net 30 days to rated firms.

6. METHOD OF ADDRESSING
4-up Cheshire. Gummed 3.50/M extra; pressure sensitive 7.00/M extra; key coding 1.25/M extra.
Magnetic tape available.

7. DELIVERY SCHEDULE
5-20 working days, usually 5 days from receipt of order.

8. RESTRICTIONS
2 sample mailing pieces must be submitted and approved prior to shipment of list.

9. TEST ARRANGEMENT
Minimum 3,000.

10. LETTER SHOP SERVICES
Complete facilities and services available in Northeastern U. S.

11. MAINTENANCE
Updated Jan., 1978.
Guaranteed 97% deliverable. Refund of .15 each on undeliverables over 3% provided that all undeliverables are returned within 30 days of mailing date. U.S.P.S. mailing receipt must be furnished with undeliverables and must indicate mailing code.

(D-C)

CULTURED NEW YORKERS

Media Code 3 600 1875 8.00
Member: D.M.M.A.
Dependable Lists, Inc., 257 Park Ave. South, New York, N. Y. 10010. Phone 212-677-6760.
For basic information on listing segments 1, 5, 6, 7, 8, 9, 11 see Dependable Lists, Inc. listing in Classification 552.

2. DESCRIPTION
Cultured New Yorkers. 85% men.
ZIP Coded in numerical sequence 100%.
List is computerized.

3. LIST SOURCE
Rosters and directories.

4. QUANTITY AND RENTAL RATES
Rec'd January, 1979.

	Total Number	Price per/M
Total list (No. 1822/C)	115,000	27.50

Selections: ZIP Code, no extra charge, keying, 1.00/M extra.
Minimum order 5,000.

DEPENDABLE'S MEMBERS OF EXCLUSIVE CLUBS

Media Code 3 600 2000 2.00
Member: D.M.M.A.
Dependable Lists, Inc., 257 Park Ave., South, New York, N. Y. 10010. Phone 212-677-6760.
For basic information on listing segments 1, 5, 6, 7, 8, 9, 11, see Dependable Lists, Inc. listing in Classification 552.

2. DESCRIPTION
Business executives and professionals who have been and country, alumni and athletic clubs members. Can address to Mr., Mrs. or Mr. & Mrs. at no extra charge. Can eliminate up to 10 states. 98% men.
ZIP Coded in numerical sequence 100%.

3. LIST SOURCE
Biographical directories.

4. QUANTITY AND RENTAL RATES
Rec'd January, 1979.

	Total Number	Price per/M
Total list (No. 5288/C)	160,000	27.50

Selections: state, SCF, 2.50/M extra; keying, 1.00/M extra.
Minimum order 3,000.

DISCRETIONARY INCOME PEOPLE

Media Code 3 600 2125 7.00
Member: D.M.M.A.
Dependable Lists, Inc., 257 Park Ave. South, New York, N Y. 10010. Phone 212-677-6760.
For basic information on listing segments 1, 5, 6, 7, 8, 9, 11 see Dependable Lists, Inc. listing in Classification 552.

2. DESCRIPTION
Educated, affluent group of executives and professionals with money to spare. 85% men.
ZIP Coded in numerical sequence 100%.

3. LIST SOURCE
Rosters and directories.

4. QUANTITY AND RENTAL RATES
Rec'd January, 1979.

	Total Number	Price per/M
Total list (No. 1024/BCM)	950,000	27.50

Selections: state, sectional center, ZIP Code, 2.50/M extra; keying 1.00/M extra.
Minimum order 5,000.

Dunhill's Social Register Families

Media Code 3 600 2250 3.00
Dunhill International List Co., Inc., 444 Park Ave. South, New York, N. Y. 10016. Phone 212-686-3700.
For basic information on the following numbered listing segments: 1, 5, 6, 7, 9 see Dunhill International List Co., Inc. listing in Classification 552.

2. DESCRIPTION
Social register families with birth date.
ZIP Coded in numerical sequence 100%.
List is computerized.

4. QUANTITY AND RENTAL RATES
Rec'd April, 1978.

	Total Number	Price per/M
Total list	55,000	30.00
Baltimore, Md.	1,400	"
Boston, Mass.	3,000	"
Brooklyn, N. Y.	2,000	"
Buffalo, N. Y.	1,100	"
Chicago, Ill.	1,700	"
Cincinnati & Dayton, Ohio	2,000	"
Cleveland, Ohio	2,000	"
Detroit, Mich.	3,200	"
New York, N. Y.	8,000	"
Palm Beach, Fla.	2,000	"
Philadelphia, Pa.	4,000	"
Pittsburgh, Pa.	1,500	"
San Francisco, Calif.	1,700	"
St. Louis, Mo.	1,800	"
Washington, D. C.	1,500	"
Junior members	10,021	"
Large estate owners	6,219	"
Socially prominent families/telephone numbers	33,800	40.00

Telephone numbers, 10.00/M extra.

11. MAINTENANCE
Updated annually.

GENTLEWOMEN

Media Code 3 600 2265 1.00
Member: D.M.M.A.
Dependable Lists, Inc., 357 Park Ave. South, New York, N. Y. 10010. Phone 212-677-6760.
For basic information on listing segments 1, 5, 6, 7, 9, 11 see the Dependable Lists, Inc. listing in Classification 552.

2. DESCRIPTION
Outstanding women in social standing and achievement in philanthropy, business, community leadership, etc.
ZIP Coded in numerical sequence 100%.

3. LIST SOURCE
Current directories.

4. QUANTITY AND RENTAL RATES
Rec'd January, 1979.

	Total Number	Price per/M
Total list (No. 4126/WC)	195,000	27.50

Selections: state, SCF, ZIP Code, 2.50/M extra; keying 1.00/M extra.
Minimum order, 3,000.

GROSSINGER GUEST LIST

Media Code 3 600 2281 8.00
Grossinger's.

1. PERSONNEL
List Manager
Hugo Dunhill Mailing Lists, Inc., 630 3rd Ave., New York, N. Y. 10017. Phone 212-682-8030.
All recognized brokers.

2. DESCRIPTION
Guests of all year round resort. High percentage in Northeast United States and Canada.

3. LIST SOURCE
Guest records of hotel.

4. QUANTITY AND RENTAL RATES
Rec'd May, 1977.

	Total Number	Price per/M
Total list (No. 9027-74-L)	124,000	30.00
Repeat guests	85,000	30.00
Last 12 months guests	27,000	35.00
Singles	12,000	40.00

Selections: state, 2.00/M extra; key code 1.00/M extra; SCF, 4.00/M extra.

6. METHOD OF ADDRESSING
Computer: 4-up Cheshire labels.
Magnetic tape available.

8. RESTRICTIONS
Submit sample mail piece for clearance.

10. LETTER SHOP SERVICES
Send orders to Hugo Dunhill.

INDIVIDUALS WITH ANNUAL INCOME OF $50,000.00 AND OVER

Media Code 3 600 2296 6.00
Member: D.M.M.A.
Dependable Lists, Inc., 257 Park Ave. South, New York, N. Y. 10010. Phone 212-677-6760.
For basic information on listing segments 1, 5, 6, 7, 8, 9, 11 see Dependable Lists, Inc., listing in Classification 552.

2. DESCRIPTION
Outstanding executives and professionals in the United States who have an annual income of 50,000.00 and over. Includes board members, trustees, top management officials of industrial and commercial firms, lawyers and other professionals. 98% men.
ZIP Coded in numerical sequence 100%.

3. LIST SOURCE
Biographic registers.

(This listing continued on next page)

Source: *Direct Mail List Rates and Data*, Consumer Lists, Standard Rate and Data Service, Inc., 5201 Old Orchard Rd., Skokie, Ill. 60077.
Sample listings from mailing list catalog.

Is there still
no room at
the inn?

FROM

_____

_____

_____

Your
first class stamp
will provide
an extra helping
of food for
a hungry
child.

THE SALVATION ARMY

P.O. BOX 14176
LANSING, MI 48901

Here's my gift to help people in need.

$100	$50	$25	$15

Yes. I want to share what I have with
others now and throughout the year.

$10	$5	Special $_____

48864 01744261 81 4561

S3LAN

THE SALVATION ARMY
P.O. BOX 14176
LANSING, MI 48901

MR THOMAS W TENBRUNSEL
2195 HERITAGE AV
OKEMOS   MI 48864

☐ Please send information on providing a life income for myself, and tax benefits

Please correct address if necessary. Make your check payable to THE SALVATION ARMY, and
return this card with your tax-deductible donation. THANK YOU!

Sample direct mail package.

"And they wrapped Him in swaddling clothes and laid Him in a manger because there was no room for them at the inn."

The Prince of Peace was born in lowly surroundings. But He became the Truth and the Light of the World.

This year, as we celebrate Christmas in the comfort of our homes, as we exchange gifts, and as love flows freely in our hearts, it is a disturbing thought to know that--

For some among us, there is still no room at the inn.

Through no fault of their own, many of God's children still suffer from a lack of food, warm clothing, a roof over their heads--and, especially at Christmas, no toys or gifts for innocent little children.

It need not be this way. If only each of us would open the door of our heart to help one another, we would make this a world of peace and good will.

The Salvation Army's most vital mission is to help others. To do this, we must come to you and ask, "Please share some of the bounty and blessings you enjoy with those less fortunate. Find room in your heart for one deserving child or family." We know who they are and will help them in your name.

Please help. Give a gift of any amount you care to share. We will turn it into food, clothing and toys for those to whom the door to the inn has been closed. What you put into the lives of others will surely come back into your own.

May God Bless You,

The Salvation Army

P.S.   Whatever you give will be used at Christmas and throughout the year to help those in need. Please mail your tax-deductible contribution today.

THANK YOU for your support of The Salvation Army through your UNITED WAY gift. This traditional CHRISTMAS PROGRAM, however, is not a part of The Salvation Army activities supported by the UNITED WAY.

Sample direct mail package.

NONPROFIT ORG.

DR. THOMAS W. TENBRUNSEL '64   T-19200
2195 HERITAGE AVENUE
OKEMOS, MICHIGAN 48864

POSTMASTER
ADDRESS CORRECTION REQUESTED
DO NOT FORWARD

NEWBURG ROAD
LOUISVILLE, KENTUCKY 40205

BELLARMINE COLLEGE

YOU CAN'T GET A BETTER RETURN ON AN INVESTMENT

At Bellarmine College, our goal is to offer only the highest quality educational programs. To accomplish this, we need your help. But we wouldn't ask you to invest your money in the College if we couldn't guarantee that every penny would be used to realize the greatest return.

NOTICE: This brochure should not be mistaken for a share of stock. Bellarmine College is a private, independent College and, as such, has no stockholders.

Sample direct mail package.

BELLARMINE COLLEGE

Dear Alum, *Dr. Tenbrunsel*

MEMORY is a powerful but fickle friend, wouldn't you agree? Most all of us remember our favorite childhood friend, our first kiss, and where we were when we heard special news. For all that we recall, however, much more is lost to us. What do you remember of your college days now? Do you recollect the name of the professor who kept you up all night cramming for that big test? Do you remember how you felt when you finally received your degree? The whole world was watching you then - at least it seemed so at the time.

Well, our school days are behind us now, but the people with whom we shared those experiences are still around. Some of them volunteered to make calls in last fall's Alumni Phon-a-thon and renewed old acquaintances while asking fellow alumni to support the College. Unfortunately, we were not able to share that experience with you, though it wasn't for lack of effort. Knowing that you have supported the College in the past, I am writing you in hopes of receiving an answer to a question our alumni volunteers were not able to ask: "Will you support Bellarmine with a donation this year?"

Why does it make sense to give to Bellarmine? Enclosed is a brochure that suggests that you consider your contribution to Bellarmine an investment in the quality of life in this community. The brochure describes the College in terms you may not remember associating with Bellarmine before. We say things like "Bellarmine is Vital to Louisville" because Bellarmine is a stable, growth-oriented institution that is serving a need in this community - a need for a top-quality private institution of higher education. As a graduate of this environment, I hope you appreciate that necessity better than anyone.

"Will my contribution really help?" You may be surprised to see how important annual giving is to Bellarmine. As the brochure illustrates, annual donations pay for roughly 14% of the College's annual operating costs. Just look inside the enclosed pledge form and you'll see what <u>your gift</u> could do. It <u>will</u> <u>make</u> <u>a</u> <u>difference</u>.

I hope that this letter and brochure answer any questions you may have had about Bellarmine's growth potential. Now I ask that you answer my question in the affirmative by again making a gift to the College. With your renewed support, Bellarmine will always be thought of as an institution that provides for the needs of its students, its alumni, and the community it serves.

Sincerely,

Steve Kirn

Steve Kirn '69
President
Bellarmine College Alumni Association

SK/11

Newburg Road · Louisville, Kentucky 40205 · 502 - 452-8011

Sample direct mail package.

77

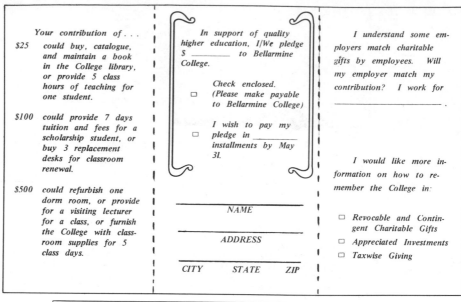

Your contribution of . . .

$25 could buy, catalogue, and maintain a book in the College library, or provide 5 class hours of teaching for one student.

$100 could provide 7 days tuition and fees for a scholarship student, or buy 3 replacement desks for classroom renewal.

$500 could refurbish one dorm room, or provide for a visiting lecturer for a class, or furnish the College with classroom supplies for 5 class days.

In support of quality higher education, I/We pledge $ _____ to Bellarmine College.

☐ *Check enclosed. (Please make payable to Bellarmine College)*

☐ *I wish to pay my pledge in _____ installments by May 31.*

NAME

ADDRESS

CITY   STATE   ZIP

I understand some employers match charitable gifts by employees. Will my employer match my contribution? I work for _____ .

I would like more information on how to remember the College in:

☐ *Revocable and Contingent Charitable Gifts*

☐ *Appreciated Investments*

☐ *Taxwise Giving*

BUSINESS REPLY MAIL
FIRST CLASS PERMIT NO. 1254, LOUISVILLE, KY.

POSTAGE WILL BE PAID BY ADDRESSEE

BELLARMINE COLLEGE
DEVELOPMENT OFFICE
2000 Norris Place
Louisville, Kentucky 40205

NO POSTAGE
NECESSARY
IF MAILED
IN THE
UNITED STATES

Sample direct mail package.

DIRECT MAIL CHECKLIST

The Outer Envelope ———▶ Get It Opened

☐ Does it resemble a bill or a "letter from Mom"?
☐ Use return address indication only if it will help to get the envelope opened.
☐ Avoid gimmicks and the sweepstakes look.
☐ Check with the post office on how much postage is required.

The Direct Mail Letter ———▶ Get It Read

☐ Letter is dated so its content has some standing in time for the reader.
☐ Salutation is personal.
☐ Grammar is intact, conversational, informal, even deviates occasionally from rules. Dictating the letter helps achieve this tone.
☐ Opening sentence is short (no more than two lines), concise, loaded with emotion.
☐ Opening paragraph captures the reader's emotion and tells what you want.
☐ Is your organization's track record clearly stated?
☐ Letter involves the reader in a real person's problem rather than boring social statistics.
☐ Uses *I* and *you*, eliminating impersonal words such as *that* and *which*.
☐ Tells the reader how he or she can help.
☐ Paragraphs are short, no longer than five or six lines.
☐ Sentences are short and to the point.
☐ Words are simple, with few words over five letters.
☐ Have you avoided overuse of underlining, capitalization, script, multiple colors which distract the reader.
☐ Have you asked readers for a gift? And explained how they can give?
☐ Does the signature on the letter have any meaning for the reader?

P.S. Always use a postscript, and since everyone always reads the postscript, it should contain your main message.

The Response Device

☐ You *must* have one
☐ Preferably separate from the envelope
☐ Simple and easy to use
☐ Contains specific categories for giving
☐ A box to check for volunteering (where appropriate)
☐ Sturdy and fits into return envelope

NOTE: Consider including your response device in your news-letter, alumni magazines, and special announcements.

The Return Envelope

☐ Opaque
☐ Preaddressed
☐ Stamped or postage paid. You should check with your local post office for details on the least expensive alternative. In general, for a mass mailing, if you expect a high response rate, use first class return postage. Use a postal permit if you expect a low response rate.
☐ Some campaigns are using "Your stamp will help," but remember the object of direct mail is to make it easy to send a gift to you.
☐ Brochure (optional). The brochure must not detract from the original intent—GIVE!

Mailing Your Direct Mail Package

☐ In determining the size of your mailing, have you taken into account
initial costs
list effectiveness
funds needed
available budget
Start small and work up to 10,000 mailings.
☐ Do you need to clear your direct mail package with the post office and the attorney general? There are many rules governing what can be sent through the mail.

EVALUATION OF YOUR DIRECT MAIL CAMPAIGN

For Eval

Every direct mail situation is unique. Even if you think you are religiously following checklists, guidelines, and procedures, you may in fact end up with a direct mail package that is ineffective. *Every* direct mail package needs to be pretested in its entirety and in terms of its various components and target audience. Direct mail campaigns cost enough money that it is worthwhile to do some prior testing to avoid a zero response rate.

In testing various aspects of direct mail packages, you will need to employ *comparative experimentation*. If you are trying to test two types of letters, you will need to select randomly a sample from your prospect list and then compare the effectiveness of the two approaches. You will need a sample large enough to give you a measurable response rate in each experimental condition. Consider the following example:

Praise Letter Mail out minimum of 400* letters.	Guilt Letter Mail out minimum of 400* letters.

Let's say you intend to mail 10,000 letters and you expect a 5 to 10 percent response rate. Because you should have a minimum of 20 returned letters in each condition, you would need to mail 800 to 1,000 letters (5 percent of 400 gives you a minimum return of 20 letters per condition. Because there are two conditions, you must mail a minimum of 800 letters in your sample).

If your prospect list numbers into the tens of thousands, you will likely be throwing away one to two thousand names depending on the number of conditions and number of pretests you decide to do. However, it is time and names well spent. I know of at least one organization which spent $10,000 on a direct mail campaign, mailed all the information without pretesting it, and received no response.

Testing Method

To determine the effectiveness of your direct mail package you will need to measure the response rate and the size and dollar

*Random assignment of names from prospect list.

amounts of donations. The response rate is a very simple index that is typically expressed as a percent of returned response devices. It helps in evaluating your package in terms of its effectiveness in generating a house list from a prospect list. The size and amount of donations are concerned with how much revenue different types of packages generate. There are two ways to look at how much revenue a particular technique generates: the size of the average gift and the total amount given.

Returning to the example above, suppose having mailed 400 copies of each letter, you obtained the following results:

	Praise Letter	*Guilt Letter*
Number of mailings	400	400
Number of responses	120	20
Response rate	30%	5%
Average gift size	$ 5	$ 35
Total amount	$600	$700

In analyzing this package, you might pick the Guilt Letter because it produced the larger total amount of dollars. However, the Praise Letter had a much larger response rate and will give you a much larger house list. The long-term benefits of the latter must be considered when deciding which letter to use.

HOW TO ASSESS LONG-RANGE EFFECTIVENESS

It is important to bear in mind that you should not concentrate exclusively on actual dollars received when evaluating alternative direct mail packages, especially if you plan to continue with future campaigns. Other considerations are list cost, mailing cost, annual solicitation, list size and stability over time, and number of years a donor will continue to donate. The problem is how to determine the effects of each of these factors on your campaign. One technique is to identify the appropriate costs and benefits of an ongoing campaign over a three- or five-year period and discount them to the present period. The formula might be something like this:

$$\sum_{t=1}^{n} \frac{\text{benefits}_t - \text{cost}_t}{(1 + \text{interest rate})^n}$$

In the formula, n is the number of time periods and t is the time period in question. You merely add the effects to reach a conclusion.

The formula would be applied over a theoretical five-year period as follows:

Mass Direct Mailing (30,000)

Period	Costs			Benefits (revenues)		
1st year	$25[a] $\times$ 30[g]		= $ 750	50[e] $\times$ 30[g] $\times$ $7[f] = $10,500		
	100[b] $\times$ 30		= $3,000	50 $\times$ 30 $\times$ $7 = $10,500		
2nd year	50[c] $\times$ 30 $\times$ $1[d]	= $1,500				
3rd year	50[c] $\times$ 30 $\times$ $1	= $1,500		50 $\times$ 30 $\times$ $7 = $10,500		
4th year	50[c] $\times$ 30 $\times$ $1	= $1,500		50 $\times$ 30 $\times$ $7 = $10,500		
5th year	50[c] $\times$ 30 $\times$ $1	= $1,500		50 $\times$ 30 $\times$ $7 = $10,500		
5-year total		= $9,750			= $52,500	

$$\sum_{t=1}^{5} \quad \frac{\$52,500 - \$9,750}{(1 + 10\%)^5} = \frac{42,750}{1.61} = \$26,553 \quad \text{net funds}[h]$$

[a] Initial list cost per 1,000.
[b] Initial mailing cost per 1,000.
[c] Donors per 1,000.
[d] Annual solicitation cost.
[e] Response rate per 1,000.
[f] Average donation.
[g] Number of thousands.
[h] Projected net amount of dollars raised over the five-year period.

Though the formula is straightforward, its application is difficult because the costs and benefits are not always easily identified. Even when identification is possible the monetary value of each will vary with the goals of the fund raising organization. Interest rates, response rates, average donations, and donor participation over time vary greatly over the business cycle and are therefore difficult to predict. In short, you should make an attempt to estimate effectiveness of your funding campaign over time, taking into effect all these factors. You should also update your estimates regularly. Above all, don't let the complexity scare you off. If it does, seek the advice of a good accountant and proceed as usual with your direct mail campaign. Ultimately, you will need to come up with a *bottom line* figure, or an estimate of how much money you can expect to raise over a number of years, when comparing two or more direct mail packages. This reinforces a previous point that direct mail is not a one-time technique, but it involves a building and continuous nurturing of house lists.

FUNDING STRATEGY PORTFOLIO

EXERCISE 1

Pick out two solicitations for fund raising from your mail, a friend's mail, or those provided in this chapter. Criticize each as a fund raising device by suggesting what you would have done differently in terms of envelope, letter, response device, and return envelope.

EXERCISE 2

Create a direct mail package for your project, including letter, envelope, response device, and return envelope.

EXERCISE 3

Develop the research design you would use to test the direct mail package you have developed and discuss what you would test, how you would test it, and the evaluation criteria you would use.

EXERCISE 4

Identify and describe one direct mail list which you would use for your initial mailing.

BIBLIOGRAPHY

ANDREWS, FRANCIS S., "The Mini-Message: Inexpensive but Effective Mail Appeals," in *Charitable Giving and Solicitation*. Englewood Cliffs, N.J.: Prentice-Hall, 1981.

BRANN, CHRISTIAN. *Direct Mail and Direct Response Promotion*. London: Kogan Page Ltd., 1971.

City Directory. R. L. Polk, 6400 Monroe Blvd., Taylor, Mich. 48180. Published annually. Available in most libraries and real estate offices. A listing of names and employment by street address.

Computer Handbook Fund-Raisers, 2nd Ed. Fund-Raising Institute, Box 122, Plymouth Meeting, Pa. 19462, 1970.

Direct Mail List Rates and Data. Standard Rate and Data Service, Inc., 5201 Old Orchard Road, Skokie, Ill. 60077, 1981.

Direct Marketing. Holse Communications, Inc. 224 7th Street, Garden City, N.Y. 11535. Monthly.

DOPPLER, WILLIAM A. *Testing: The Scientific Approach to Direct Mail*. New York: Direct Mail Advertising Association, 1960.

GRUBB, DAVID L. and DAVID R. ZWICH. "A Citizen's Guide to Direct Mail Fund-Raising." Fund-Raising in the Public Interest, P.O. Box 19367, Washington, D.C. 20036, 1976.

HODGSON, RICHARD S. *Direct Mail and Mail Order Handbook.* The Dartnell Corporation, 4660 North Ravenswood, Chicago, Ill. 60640, 1974.

HOKE, HENRY REED. *What You Should Know About Direct Mail.* New York: Oceana Publications, 1966.

KELLER, MITCHELL. *The KRC Guide to Direct Mail Fund Raising.* Public Service Materials Center, 355 Lexington Avenue, New York, N.Y. 10017, 1977.

The KRC Manual of Computer Applications in Fund-Raising. KRC Associates, 105 Mamaroneck Avenue, Mamaroneck, N.Y. 10543, 1972.

MARTYN, SEAN. *How to Start and Run a Successful Mail Order Business.* New York: David McKay Company, Inc., 1969.

MAYER, EDWARD N., and ROY G. LJUNGREN. *Handbook of Industrial Direct Mail Advertising.* Association of Industrial Advertisers, 41 East 42nd Street, New York, N.Y. 10017, 1972.

PETERSON, ELIZABETH BRODER. *Spend Less, Raise More: A Cost-Conscious Look at Direct Mail Fund-Raising.* Direct Mail Fund-Raising Association, 810 7th Avenue, New York, N.Y. 10106, 1974.

Postal Manual. U.S. Postal Service. Available in all post offices.

The World Almanac and Book of Facts. Newspaper Enterprise Association, New York, N.Y. Zip code list of every town in the United States with 5,000 or more people. Published annually.

QUIZ

Answer true or false.

1. The good direct mail package includes an outer envelope, a letter, a response device, and a return envelope. A brochure is optional.
2. It is usually to your advantage to rent a direct mail list from a list owner rather than a list broker.
3. A prospect list contains the names of people who contribute regularly to your nonprofit organization.
4. You spent $1,000 on your first direct mail campaign and got back $1,000 in donations. It wasn't worth it.
5. Direct mail is an easy and inexpensive way for nonprofit organizations to raise start-up funds.

6. You should always include a postscript in a direct mail package.

7. Always incorporate a testing design with your direct mail campaign to help you increase your success and avoid a zero response rate.

8. Your best possible mailing list is your house list.

9. A good direct mail letter should be a "conversation with the reader."

10. In your DIRECT MAIL LETTER underscore and *capitalize* ALL the "important" points for *maximum* effect!

Chapter 6

GOVERNMENT FUNDING

Government funding, government grantsmanship, is perhaps the most popular of all the methods of fund raising. Most organizations have at some time or another considered, applied for, or received a government grant. On the other hand, if you are in the arts or humanities, you are probably wondering how to get your first government grant.

There are more myths associated with government funding than any other source of funding. Lengthy proposals and bureaucracy have scared many organizations away from an otherwise solid source of program monies. Although not as readily as in the 1960s, the government still gives money away. In fact, it continues to give more money away each year, but the increasing competition for funds creates the net effect of fewer available dollars per agency. Inflation and cutbacks in federal spending will increase the competition for grants. Your organization will be competing with long-standing institutions in the community (hospitals, universities) for available funds. New starts and many old programs will yield to program maintenance. You must, therefore, sharpen your skills at identifying government funding programs, matching your interest to theirs, and asking for government funds (proposal writing).

This chapter will help you to search systematically the volumes of government programs and provide helpful hints throughout. Before you begin, make a *key words list* of five or so words which describe your project. Look for the obscure as well as the sure-fire government source. Learn how to use the *Catalogue of Federal Domestic Assistance*. It is the bible of government funding. Plan to spend more hours than ever reading and researching government material, because one thing is certain, the government publishes more than any other entity. Locate the government depository library nearest you. Then chalk up some days paging through catalogs, directories, newsletters, announcements, laws, hearings, and transcripts until you find the "right" agency.

You will need to keep in tune with what is happening in government. Cultivate the people in government: legislators, their staffs, and agency staff. Even in government, the saying "people give to people" holds true. The cultivation process may not be the same as with the individual giver or corporate president; but remember, it is the government "bureaucrat" who knows "tomorrow's priorities," and tomorrow's priorities are the substance of today's proposals. And, oh yes, do not try to change those government priorities—change yours.

If you are wondering whether or not to get political in the grants process, a good rule of thumb is not to if you can avoid it. Congressional meddling in behalf of your project can backfire. However, if you continue to get aced out by the mayor of another city, it's time to get tough. In the final analysis, you must use your own discretion.

Proposal writing continues to take a back seat to developing your funding strategy. A good proposal will not guarantee funding, but a bad one will guarantee no funding. Today most proposals are very good. It is, therefore, the unique proposal that gets funded. The resourceful grantsperson uses a well-prepared, well-written proposal first as a formal request for funds, second as a tool to negotiate with the funding agency, and finally as a managerial tool once the grant is accepted. After the needs have been carefully identified, objectives laid out, and methods agreed upon, you are ready to sit down and dictate the technically competent proposal. The trend is away from colossal proposals in government. This chapter suggests, particularly in regard to an unsolicited proposal (one for which the funding agency has issued no strict format or guidelines), that you avoid dull, lengthy proposals and prepare a neatly organized, concise, well-written ten-page proposal. The proposal checklist will help you increase your fundability score before you submit your proposal. The most difficult step in proposal writing is the first draft. You then have something that people can react to and refine into final form.

This chapter is designed to move you through the proposal writing process to a proposal outline and a first draft. Use the worksheets provided to facilitate this process.

Government fund raising flow chart.

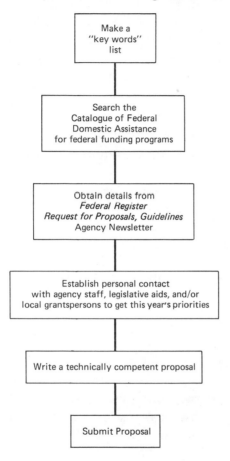

TYPES OF GRANTS

Block   Grant to a state or local communities for broad purposes. There is flexibility in what is funded as long as the broad purpose is fulfilled. Usually private nonprofit organizations apply to the state or local community government for funds.

Categorical	Grant made for a specific purpose.
Construction	Grant to support building, expanding, or renovating.
Demonstration	Grant made to establish the feasibility of a program idea.
Developmental	Grant made to establish a new or innovative program as part of the system.
Discretionary	Grant made in support of a project solely at the discretion of the granting agency, usually from the Secretary or departmental head.
Planning	Grant made to support planning, developing, or designing a program or research project.
Research	Grant made in support of experimental research.
Service	Grant made to provide or expand a service such as health or transportation.
Staffing	Grant to provide staff salaries to an institution or agency.
Training	Grant made to train students, staff, and other personnel in research or technical skills.

There are other less commonly referred to grants: capitation, conference, consortium, continuing education, formula. A description of these and others can be found in Virginia White's book, *Grants.**

SOURCES OF INFORMATION
ON GOVERNMENT FUNDING†

CATALOGUE OF FEDERAL DOMESTIC ASSISTANCE
Begin here. The current catalog is available in the library or your local congressperson's office. It contains information on every government funding program, program objectives, types of assistance, uses and restrictions, eligibility requirements, application and award process, size of grant assistance, person to contact, and related programs. It is conveniently indexed by agency name, subject area, and several other helpful indices. Make up a *key words* list for your project; then proceed by using the *catalogue's* access numbers to exhaust all possible sources. Pay

*New York: Plenum Publishing Corp., 1976, pp. 293-294.
†See sample entries from these sources on the pages that follow.

particular attention to the related programs category in each listing for further leads.

FEDERAL ASSISTANCE PROGRAMS RETRIEVAL SYSTEM (FAPRS)

FAPRS could be a ready source of information on government programs, funding, and priorities, but more recently it has fallen prey to hapless government bureaucracy. The 1978 law intended FAPRS to be a super, up-to-the-minute system, accessible to all citizens at low cost. So far nothing has happened, but there is hope in the bureaucratic phoenix.

FEDERAL REGISTER

The *Federal Register*, a daily publication, is elaborately indexed and cross-referenced; ask your librarian to help you. All federal grant programs must appear here before any grant is awarded. Check it regularly.

COMMERCE BUSINESS DAILY

Similar to the *Federal Register* but deals mainly with contract requests and announcements.

OTHER SOURCES OF INFORMATION

Program announcements/requests for proposals (RFPS).

Agency publications, newsletters, annual reports, special reports (get on the mailing list).

Congressional hearings and legislation. (You need to know the intent of the legislation associated with the funding program. Use the *Catalogue of Federal Domestic Assistance* and the *Federal Register* and your librarian to identify and track down authorizing legislation.)

Funding agency staff (your best source for up-to-date priorities).

Congressional staff members.

Local grants office or funding resource center.

Federal Assistance Programs Retrieval System (FAPRS) Input Categories

1. COMMUNITY FACILITIES
    1. Community water supply
    2. Community sewage treatment
    3. Solid waste management
    4. Public buildings
    5. Hospitals and health-related facilities
    6. Recreation

AGENCY PROGRAM INDEX

Program Description	Financial	Non-Financial	Combined

The alphabet(s) in parentheses following the program title, shows the type(s) of assistance available through that program. The alphabet codes with accompanying types of assistance are as follows: A—Formula Grants; B—Project Grants; C—Direct Payments for Specified Use; D—Direct Payments with Unrestricted Use; E—Direct Loans; F—Guaranteed/Insured Loans; G—Insurance; H—Sale, Exchange, or Donation of Property and Goods; I—Use of Property, Facilities, and Equipment; J—Provision of Specialized Services; K—Advisory Services and Counseling; L—Dissemination of Technical Information; M—Training; N—Investigation of Complaints; O—Federal Employment.

Included in the Agency Program Index Is a chart to help users distinguish programs that provide financial assistance from those providing services and technical assistance. There is also a column included which lists those programs that provide both financial and non-financial assistance.

DEPARTMENT OF AGRICULTURE

ANIMAL AND PLANT HEALTH INSPECTION SERVICE

Program Description	Financial	Non-Financial	Combined
10.025 Plant and Animal Disease and Pest Control (J,L)		X	

AGRICULTURAL STABILIZATION AND CONSERVATION SERVICE

Program Description	Financial	Non-Financial	Combined
10.051 Commodity Loans and Purchases (D,E)	X		
10.052 Cotton Production Stabilization (D)	X		
10.053 Dairy Indemnity Payments (D)	X		
10.054 Emergency Conservation Program (C)	X		
10.055 Feed Grain Production Stabilization (D)	X		
10.056 Storage Facilities and Equipment Loans (E)	X		
10.058 Wheat Production Stabilization (D)	X		
10.059 National Wool Act Payments (D)	X		
10.060 Beekeeper Indemnity Payments (D)	X		
10.062 Water Bank Program (C)	X		
10.063 Agricultural Conservation Program (C)	X		
10.064 Forestry Incentives Program (C)	X		
10.065 Rice Production Stabilization (D)	X		
10.066 Emergency Feed Program (D)	X		
10.067 Grain Reserve Program (D)	X		
10.068 Rural Clean Water Program (C)	X		

AGRICULTURAL MARKETING SERVICE

Program Description	Financial	Non-Financial	Combined
10.150 Agricultural Product Grading (J)		X	
10.153 Market News (L)		X	
10.154 Market Supervision (J,K,M,N)		X	
10.155 Marketing Agreements and Orders (J,K)		X	
10.156 Federal—State Marketing Improvement Program (B)	X		
10.159 Livestock and Poultry Market Supervision (N)		X	

ECONOMICS, STATISTICS, AND COOPERATIVES SERVICE

Program Description	Financial	Non-Financial	Combined
10.250 Agricultural and Rural Economic Research (L)		X	
10.251 Technical Assistance to Cooperatives (K,L)		X	
10.252 Agriculture Statistical Reports (L)		X	

FARMERS HOME ADMINISTRATION

Program Description	Financial	Non-Financial	Combined
10.404 Emergency Loans (F)	X		
10.405 Farm Labor Housing Loans and Grants (B,F)	X		
10.406 Farm Operating Loans (F)	X		
10.407 Farm Ownership Loans (F)	X		
10.408 Grazing Association Loans (F)	X		
10.409 Irrigation, Drainage, and Other Soil and Water Conservation Loans (F)	X		
10.410 Low to Moderate Income Housing Loans (F)	X		
10.411 Rural Housing Site Loans (E,F)	X		
10.413 Recreation Facility Loans (F)	X		
10.414 Resource Conservation and Development Loans (F)	X		
10.415 Rural Rental Housing Loans (F)	X		
10.416 Soil and Water Loans (F)	X		
10.417 Very Low—Income Housing Repair Loans and Grants (B,E)	X		
10.418 Water and Waste Disposal Systems for Rural Communities (B,F)	X		
10.419 Watershed Protection and Flood Prevention Loans (F)	X		
10.420 Rural Self—Help Housing Technical Assistance (B)	X		
10.421 Indian Tribes and Tribal Corporation Loans (F)	X		
10.422 Business and Industrial Loans (F)	X		

Catalogue of Federal Domestic Assistance.

alcohol, tobacco, and firearms police instruction, 21.052
crime control, comprehensive plan implementation, 16.532
development of criminal justice programs in colleges and universities, 16.533
FBI advanced police training, 16.300
FBI crime laboratory, 16.301
FBI field police training, 16.302
FBI National Academy, 16.300
faculty training, 16.533
fellowships, research and development, 16.541, 16.542
graduate research fellowships, 16.625
narcotics and dangerous drugs, 16.004
professional improvement, 16.534
project grants, research and development, 16.540
safe streets, comprehensive plan implementation, 16.532
safe streets, comprehensive planning assistance, 16.530
safe streets, crime control, 16.530, 16.531, 16.532
safe streets, discretionary grants, 16.531
secret service training activities, 21.100
seminars, workshops, conferences, 16.534
State conservation officers in criminal law, 15.602
training for judges, judicial personnel, probation and parole personnel, welfare workers, ex-offenders, paraprofessionals, 16.601
Visiting Fellowship Program, 16.541
Libraries, general
    agricultural, 10.883
    college and university libraries, 13.406
    depository libraries, government publications, 40.001
    Distribution of Library of Congress Cataloging, 42.003
    humanities program development, 45.113
    interlibrary cooperation, 13.465
    librarian training, 13.468, 13.475
    library and archival collections in the humanities, 45.124
    library institute and fellowship program, 13.468
    National Archives reference services, 39.004
    rare resource materials for research in humanities, 45.124
    research and demonstration project, 13.475
    school library assistance, 13.570
    Smithsonian Institution Libraries, 60.001
    strengthening research library resources, 13.576
Library of Congress
    books for the blind, 42.001
    catalog cards, distribution, 42.003
    copyright service, 42.002
    national referral center for science and technology, 42.007
    preservation, restoration, and protection of library publications, 42.005
    Quarterly Journal of Collections and Programs, 42.005
    reference and bibliographic services, 42.006
    research and referral, science and technology, 42.007
    specialized reference and bibliographic services, 42.006
Low-income persons and families
    comprehensive employment and training, 17.232
    day care, Title XX social services, 13.642
    Food Distribution, 10.550
    Food Stamps, 10.551
    Head Start, 13.600
    housing repair loans, 10.417
    Medicaid, 13.714
    mini-grants to public and private organizations, 72.010
    small business loans, 59.003
    Title XX social services, 13.642
    work incentives programs, 13.646
Low or moderate income housing
    above-moderate income housing loans, 10.429
    acquisition, construction, rehabilitation, loans and grants, 14.146
    Appalachia housing, 23.005
    cooperative and multifamily housing, correcting physical deficiencies, 14.164

correcting physical deficiencies, cooperative and multi-family housing, 14.164
default, delinquency and comprehensive homeownership and financial counseling, 10.431
Emergency Energy Conservation Services, 49.014, 81.042
homeownership opportunities, 14.147
housing assistance payments, 14.156
housing development, assistance to neighborhood organizations, 14.800
interest subsidies, 14.103
low or moderate income families, 14.103, 14.120, 14.135, 14.137
minor home improvement loans and grants, 10.417
multifamily housing, 14.135, 14.137, 14.149, 14.164
neighborhood conservation and rehabilitation, 14.800
nonprofit sponsors, direct interest-free loans, 14.141
outreach, housing development and delivery, 10.431
reducing operating deficit, assisting troubled projects, 14.164
rent supplements, 14.149
rental and cooperative housing, 14.137
rural loans, 10.410, 10.417
rural rental assistance, 10.427
Section 236, 14.103
self-help loans to nonprofit organizations to aid low-income, 10.411
technical assistance for developing multiple family housing projects, 10.431
Turnkey, 14.147
winterizing repairs for low-income and elderly, 49.014, 81.042
Low or moderate income housing mortgages
    cooperative housing, loan insurance, interest subsidies, 14.103
    cooperative or rental housing, 14.137
    housing in older declining areas, 14.123
    loan insurance, 14.120
    rental housing loan insurance, 14.135
    rental housing, loan insurance, interest subsidies, 14.103
Livestock industry
    animal damage control, 15.601
    emergency feed, 10.066
    farm emergency loans, 10.404
    Grazing Association Loans, 10.408
    improving health and productivity of food animals, prevention, control, treatment of disease, research, 10.885
    protection of human health through control of animal diseases transmitted to humans, 10.885
    research, 10.876
    unfair business practices, 10.159

M

Maps and charts
    census, statistical areas, 11.003
    geodetic control surveys, 11.400
    geodetic information, 15.801
    maps of States, counties, congressional districts, 11.003
    mineral resources, 15.800
    nautical charts and related data, 11.401
    Standard Metropolitan Statistical Area maps, 11.003
    the Congressional District Atlas, 11.003
    topographic mapping, 15.803
Marine sciences
    Coast Guard cooperative program, 20.002
    sea-grant program, 11.417
Maritime industries
    complaints, 33.001
    Longshoremen's and Harbor Workers' Compensation Act, 17.302
    maritime war risk insurance, 11.503
    unfair practices investigation, 33.001
Maternal and child health
    Appalachia, 23.004, 23.013
    child health research grants, 13.231
    child welfare and development research, 13.608

Catalogue of Federal Domestic Assistance.

93

RELATED PROGRAMS: 10.063, Agricultural Conservation Program; 10.409, Irrigation, Drainage, and Other Soil and Water Conservation Loans; 10.419, Watershed Protection and Flood Prevention Loans; 10.881, Cooperative Extension Service; 10.902, Soil and Water Conservation; 15.124, Indian Loans Economic Development.

EXAMPLES OF FUNDED PROJECTS: Not applicable.

CRITERIA FOR SELECTING PROPOSALS: Not applicable.

10.417 VERY LOW-INCOME HOUSING REPAIR LOANS AND GRANTS

(Section 504 Housing Loans and Grants)

FEDERAL AGENCY: FARMERS HOME ADMINISTRATION, DEPARTMENT OF AGRICULTURE

AUTHORIZATION: Housing Act of 1949, as amended, Section 504; Public Laws 89-117, 89-754, and 92-310; 42 U.S.C. 1474.

OBJECTIVES: To give very low-income rural homeowners an opportunity to make essential repairs to their homes to make them safe and to remove health hazards to the family or the community.

TYPES OF ASSISTANCE: Direct Loans; Project Grants.

USES AND USE RESTRICTIONS: To assist owner-occupants in rural areas who do not qualify for Section 502 loans to repair or improve their dwellings in order to make such dwellings safe and sanitary and to remove hazards to the health of the occupants, their families, or the community. This includes repairs to the foundation, roof or basic structure as well as water and waste disposal systems, and weatherization. Restrictions: Maximum loan assistance of $7,500 and maximum grant assistance of $5,000 to any person for home improvement, however, maximum grant assistance must not exceed $5,000 in a loan/grant combination; loans and grants may not be made to assist in the construction of new dwellings; and, the housing must be located in a place which is rural in character and does not exceed 10,000 population or in a place whose population exceeds 10,000 but is not in excess of 20,000, provided the place is not a Standard Metropolitan Statistical Area and has a serious lack of mortgage credit for low- and moderate-income families as determined by the Secretary of Agriculture and the Secretary of Housing and Urban Development.

ELIGIBILITY REQUIREMENTS:

Applicant Eligibility: Applicant must own and occupy a home in a rural area; be without sufficient income to qualify for a Section 502 loan; have sufficient income to repay the loan; and be a citizen of the U.S. or reside in the U.S. after having been legally admitted for permanent residence or on indefinite parole. Grant recipients must be 62 years of age or older and be unable to repay the part of the assistance received as a grant. Assistance is available in States, Puerto Rico, Virgin Islands, Guam, American Samoa, the Northern Marianas, and the Trust Territory of the Pacific Islands.

Beneficiary Eligibility: Same as Applicant Eligibility.

Credentials/Documentation: Evidence of ownership and verification of income and debts.

APPLICATION AND AWARD PROCESS:

Preapplication Coordination: None.

Application Procedure: Application form obtainable from the local FmHA offices.

Award Procedure: Delegated to County Supervisor.

Deadlines: None.

Range of Approval/Disapproval Time: From 30 to 60 days from time applications is filed if no backlog of applications exists.

Appeals: Applicant may request reconsideration at the local County Office or may appeal to the State or National Office any adverse action on his loan application in accordance with FmHA appeal procedure. Appeals may be filed within 30 days after notification of the adverse decision is received by the loan or grant applicant.

Renewals: Applicants may reapply at any time.

ASSISTANCE CONSIDERATIONS:

Formula and Matching Requirements: No matching of funds required. The following formula is used to allocate program loan funds to various States: (B x .50 C x .50)x funds available = State allocation. Where "B" is State's percentage of national rural population

living in dwellings which lack complete plumbing and/or are crowded; and "C" is State's percentage of national rural population below poverty level. The formula for grants is: (B x .33 C x .33 E x .33)x funds available = State allocation. Where "E" is State's percentage of national rural population 62 years of age and over.

Length and Time Phasing of Assistance: Refinancing is required when the borrower has obtained adequate resources to finance on his own account the necessary housing or is able to secure the necessary credit from other sources on terms and conditions which he can reasonably be expected to fulfill.

POST ASSISTANCE REQUIREMENTS:

Reports: None.

Audits: As requested.

Records: Kept for outstanding loans and grants. Records retired in accordance with pertinent FmHA regulations.

FINANCIAL INFORMATION:

Account Identification: (Loans) 12-4141-0-3-371; (Grants) 12-2064-0-1-604.

Obligations: (Loans) FY 79 $14,710,250; FY 80 est $24,000,000; and FY 81 est $50,000,000. (Grants) FY 79 $18,999,980; FY 80 est $24,000,000; and FY 81 est $25,000,000.

Range and Average of Financial Assistance: Loans-$200 to $5,000; $2,630; Grants-$200 to $5,000; $2,777.

PROGRAM ACCOMPLISHMENTS: (Loans made) 5,651 in fiscal year 1979; an estimated 8,500 in fiscal year 1980; and an estimated 16,000 in fiscal year 1981. (Grants made) 6,842 in fiscal year 1979; an estimated 8,000 in fiscal year 1980; and an estimated 7,535 in fiscal year 1981.

REGULATIONS, GUIDELINES, AND LITERATURE: 7 CFR 1822.21-1822.33; FmHA Instruction 1904-G "Section 504 Rural Housing Loans and Grants" (no charge); Home Improvement and Repair Loans, PA-1184, no charge.

INFORMATION CONTACTS:

Regional or Local Office: Consult your local telephone directory for FmHA county office number. If no listing, get in touch with appropriate FmHA State office listed in Appendix IV.

Headquarters Office: Administrator, Farmers Home Administration, Department of Agriculture, Washington, DC 20250. Telephone: (202) 447-7967 (Use same 7-digit number for FTS).

RELATED PROGRAMS: 10.410, Low to Moderate Income Housing Loans; 14.108, Rehabilitation Mortgage Insurance; 14.142, Property Improvement Loan Insurance for Improving All Existing Structures and Building of New Nonresidential Structures.

EXAMPLES OF FUNDED PROJECTS: Not presently available.

CRITERIA FOR SELECTING PROPOSALS: Not presently available.

10.418 WATER AND WASTE DISPOSAL SYSTEMS FOR RURAL COMMUNITIES

FEDERAL AGENCY: FARMERS HOME ADMINISTRATION, DEPARTMENT OF AGRICULTURE

AUTHORIZATION: Consolidated Farm and Rural Development Act, Section 306; Public Law 92-419; 7 U.S.C. 1926.

OBJECTIVES: To provide basic human amenities, alleviate health hazards and promote the orderly growth of the rural areas of the nation by meeting the need for new and improved rural water and waste disposal facilities.

TYPES OF ASSISTANCE: Project Grants; Guaranteed/Insured Loans.

USES AND USE RESTRICTIONS: Funds may be used for the installation, repair, improvement, or expansion of a rural water facility including distribution lines, well pumping facilities and costs related thereto, and the installation, repair, improvement, or expansion of a rural waste disposal facility including the collection, and treatment of sanitary, storm, and solid wastes. Grant funds may not be used to pay: interest on loans, operations and maintenance costs, or to acquire or refinance an existing system. No maximum loan amount is established by statute. The maximum term on all

Catalogue of Federal Domestic Assistance.

    7. Land acquisition
    8. Public roads and bridges
    9. Utilities
  10. Historic preservation
  11. Federal surplus property
  12. Flood prevention and control
  13. Emergency preparedness and disaster relief
  14. Fire protection
  15. Research and development

2. BUSINESS AND INDUSTRIAL DEVELOPMENT
    1. Operating capital assistance
    2. Construction and equipment assistance
    3. Small business
    4. Site acquisition
    5. Environmental health and safety compliance
    6. Economic injury and natural disaster
    7. Minority business enterprise
    8. Research and development

3. PLANNING AND TECHNICAL ASSISTANCE
    1. Data and information
    2. Community facilities
    3. Business and industrial development
    4. Natural resources
    5. Agriculture
    6. Human resources
    7. Transportation
    8. Education
    9. Housing

4. HOUSING
    1. Construction or purchase of structures for private housing
    2. Construction or purchase of structures for public housing
    3. Repair, improvement, or rehabilitation on housing structures
    4. Rental or leasing supplements, mortgage assistance payments
    5. Land acquisition
    6. Site preparation for housing
    7. Property or mortgage insurance
    8. Research and development

5. EDUCATION
    1. Curriculum
    2. Demonstration
    3. Emergency assistance

4. Facilities, planning, construction and equipment
5. Libraries and related information services
6. Planning and technical assistance
7. Program development
8. Resource development and support
9. Scholarship and other financial assistance
10. Training
11. Research and development

6. EMPLOYMENT

1. Facilities planning, construction and equipment
2. Information services
3. Job placement and creation
4. Occupational safety and health
5. Planning and technical assistance
6. Program development
7. Services
8. Training and education
9. Research and development

7. HEALTH

1. Demonstration
2. Education and training
3. Emergency and disaster
4. Facilities planning, construction, and equipment
5. Information services
6. Occupational safety and health
7. Planning and technical assistance
8. Prevention and control
9. Program development
10. Services
11. Research and development

8. SOCIAL SERVICES

1. Demonstration
2. Emergency and crisis assistance
3. Family and child services
4. Home services
5. Information and referral services
6. Legal and advocacy services
7. Nutrition
8. Prevention
9. Recreation and physical fitness
10. Rehabilitation
11. Training
12. Research and development

TABLE OF CONTENTS

ATTACHMENTS

A.   Variables for Descriptive Profiles and Evaluability Assessments,
     consisting of 1 page.
B.   Nutrition Education and Training (NET) Program State Funding Levels
     and Estimated Target Population Size, consisting of 3 pages.
C.   Contract Pricing Proposal, OF 60, consisting of 3 pages.*
D.   Certificate of Current Cost and Pricing Data, consisting of 1 page.

     * Offerors must complete these sections

Sample request for proposal.

federal register

Tuesday
December 9, 1980

Highlights

81030 **Food Stamps** USDA/FNS publishes emergency
rulemaking amending the Food Stamp Program
Performance Reporting System regulations by
establishing quality control procedures; effective
8–1–80; comments by 2–9–81

81058 **Nuclear Waste** NRC proposes amending
regulations regarding advance notification to States
of transportation of certain types of nuclear waste;
comments by 3–9–81

81047 **Scholarships** Harry S. Truman Scholarship
Foundation amends regulations governing the
annual competition for scholarships; effective
12–15–80

81089 **Grant Programs** Commerce/MBDA solicits
applicants for four projects at up to total cost of
$835,000 to provide management and technical
assistance to minority-owned businesses; apply by
1–8–81

81126 **Grant Programs—Health** HHS/HRA announces
acceptance of applications for Allied Health
Professions Traineeship Grants for Advanced
Training; apply by 2–6–81

CONTINUED INSIDE

98

Administration will take such action as may be deemed appropriate.

In the event petitions regarding the relevant section 805(a) issues are received from parties with standing to be heard, a hearing will be held, the purpose of which will be to receive evidence under section 805(a) relative to whether the proposed operations (a) could result in unfair competition to any person, firm, or corporation operating exclusively in the coastwise or intercoastal service, or (b) would be prejudicial to the objects and policy of the Act.

(Catalog of Federal Domestic Assistance Program No. 11.504 Operating-Differential Subsidies (ODS))

By order of the Assistant Secretary for Maritime Affairs.

Date: December 3, 1980.

Robert J. Patton, Jr.,
Secretary.

[FR Doc. 80–38040 Filed 12–8–80; 8:45 am]
BILLING CODE 3510–15–M

Minority Business Development Agency

Financial Assistance Application Announcement

The Minority Business Development Agency announces that it is seeking applications under its program to operate four New York Region projects for a twelve month period beginning April 1, 1981. The aggregate total cost of the projects is $835,000.

Funding Instrument: It is anticipated that the funding instruments, as defined by the Federal Grant and Cooperative Agreements Act of 1977, will be grants.

Program Description: The General Business Services Program of the Minority Business Development Agency (MBDA) provides technical assistance without charge to eligible minority business persons and minority-owned firms for the purpose of improving their stability by increasing their management and marketing capabilities. MBDA offers competitive grants to consulting firms (either "not for profit" or commercial entities). These firms must be capable of providing such services as preparation of business plans, financial analysis, industrial management assistance, personnel management services, marketing planning and a broad range of other business services excluding legal services.

Applications are invited for the following four projects:

1. One grant for a management and technical assistance project to operate in the Bronx and Putnam and Rockland and Westchester Counties of New York

State. The Project will operate at a cost not to exceed $220,000. The Project I. D. Number is 02–10–80002–01.

2. One grant for a management and technical assistance project to operate in the entire State of Connecticut. The Project will operate at a cost not to exceed $165,000. The Project I. D. Number is 01–10–80005–01.

3. One grant for a management and technical assistance project to operate in the Northern Section of New Jersey. The Project will operate at a cost not to exceed $285,000. The Project I. D. Number is 02–10–80004–01.

4. One grant for a management and technical assistance project to operate in the entire State of New Jersey. Only construction contractors will be served under this project. The Project will operate at a cost not to exceed $165,000. The Project I. D. Number is 02–10–80008–01.

Eligibility Requirements: There are no restrictions. Any profit or non-profit institution is eligible to submit an application.

Application Materials: An application kit for these projects may be requested by writing to the following address: U.S. Department of Commerce, Minority Business Development Agency, Grants Administration Unit, 26 Federal Plaza, Room #3707, New York, New York 10278.

In requesting an application kit, the applicant must specify its profit status; i.e., State or local government, Federally recognized Indian tribal units, educational institutions, or other type of profit or non-profit institution. This information is necessary to enable MBDA to include the appropriate cost principles in the application kit.

Award Process: All applications that are submitted in accordance with the instructions in the application kit will be submitted to a panel for review and ranking. Specific criteria by which applications will be evaluated is included in the application kit.

Closing Date: Applicants are encouraged to obtain an application kit as soon as possible in order to allow sufficient time to prepare and submit an application before the closing date of January 8, 1981. Applications received after that date will not be considered. A pre-application conference will be held on Monday, December 22, 1980 at 2:00 PM at 26 Federal Plaza, Room #305B, New York City. Detailed submission procedures are outlined in each application kit.

(Catalog of Federal Domestic Assistance, 11.800 Minority Business Development)

Note.—This program is not subject to the requirements of OMB Circular A–95.

Dated: December 2, 1980.

Carlton L. Eccles,
Regional Director.

[FR Doc. 80–38137 Filed 12–8–80; 8:45 am]
BILLING CODE 3510–21–M

National Bureau of Standards

Availability of Calibration Transfer Specimens for Insulation

The National Bureau of Standards (NBS) announces a program for making available on request measured calibration transfer specimens for use in conjunction with the "representative thickness" provision of the Federal Trade Commission (FTC) rules on "Labeling and Advertising of Home Insulation," 16 CFR 460.6. The representative thickness testing provison of the rule, section 460.6. The representative thickness testing provision of the rule, section 460.6, was temporarily stayed until such time as these materials are available from NBS (45 FR 54702, August 15, 1980). The calibration transfer specimens are for use with apparatus that conform to the testing methods given in the American Society for Testing and Materials (ASTM), C–177–76, Standard Test Method for Steady-State Thermal Transmission Properties by Means of the Guarded Hot-Plate, and C–518–76, Standard Test Method for Steady-State Thermal Transmission Properties by Means of the Heat-Flow Meter. The specimens will be measured at a mean temperature of about 24°C (75°F) and a temperature difference of 28°C (50°F) with heat flow up for a one-sided apparatus and heat flow up and down for a two-sided apparatus. The specimens will be available at thicknesses of about 25 mm (1-inch), 75 mm (3-inch), and 150 mm (6-inch), and of a size up to a maximum diameter of about 1000 mm (40-inch) with matching masks available to give 1200 mm square (48-inch) configuration.

These specimens will be distributed by NBS through its Office of Energy Programs. The order form and price list available from this Office give further details as well as the sample test report that will accompany each specimen.

It should be noted that the cut-off date for receipt of orders for the first concurrent distribution of specimens to a group of laboratories is January 5, 1981. A second announcement after January 5, 1981, will give the distribution date and other pertinent information. This second announcement will be published in the *Commerce Business Daily* and the **Federal Register.**

Office of Human Development Services

White House Conference on Aging; Technical Committee Meeting

The White House Conference on Aging Technical Committee was established to provide scientific and technical advice and recommendations to the National Advisory Committee of the 1981 White House Conference on Aging and to the Executive Director of the 1981 White House Conference on Aging in developing issues to be considered and to produce technical documents to be used by the Conference.

Notice is hereby given pursuant to the Federal Advisory Committee Act, (Pub. L. 92–463, 5 U.S.C. App. 1, sec. 10, 1976) that the Technical Committee on Age-Integrated Society: Education will hold their next meeting on Monday, December 15, 1980 from 9:00 a.m. until 4:30 p.m. in Room 403–A, Hubert H. Humphrey Building, 200 Independence Avenue, S.W., Washington, D.C. 20201.

The purpose of the meeting will be to review final slate of concerns to be included in the final Education Technical Committee Report.

Further information on the Technical Committee meeting may be obtained from Mr. Jerome R. Waldie, Executive Director, White House Conference on Aging, Room 4059, 330 Independence Avenue, S.W., Washington, D.C. 20201, telephone (202) 245–1914. Technical Committee meetings are open for public observation.

This meeting notice did not meet the 15-day submission deadline due to difficulty in securing Federal meeting space.

Dated: December 3, 1980.

Mamie Welborne,
HDS Committee Management Officer.
[FR Doc. 80–38076 Filed 12–8–80; 8:45 am]
BILLING CODE 4110–92–M

National Institutes of Health

Bioassays of a Mixture of 1,2,3,6,7,8-Hexachlorodibenzo-p-Dioxin and 1,2,3,7,8,9-Hexachlorodibenzo-p-Dioxin (Gavage and Dermal Studies) for Possible Carcinogenicity; Availability

1,2,3,6,7,8-Hexachlorodibenzo-p-dioxin and 1,2,3,7,8,9-Hexachlorodibenzo-p-dioxin (Gavage and Dermal Studies) (CAS 57653–85–7 and CAS 19408–74–3) have been tested for cancer-causing activity with rats and mice in the Biosassay Program of the National Toxicology Program. Reports are available to the public.

Summary of Gavage Study: A

bioassay of a mixture of 1,2,3,6,7,8- and 1,2,3,7,8,9-hexachlorodibenzo-p-dioxin (HCDD) for possible carcinogenity was conducted by administering the test material by gavage to Osborne-Mendel rats and B6C3F1 mice for 104 weeks.

Under the conditions of this bioassay, HCDD administered by gavage was carcinogenic, causing increased incidences of hepatocellular carcinomas or neoplastic nodules in female Osborne-Mendel rats and inducing hepatocellular carcinomas and adenomas in male and female B6CF1 mice. HCDD was not demonstrated to be caricinogenic for male rats.

Summary of Dermal Study: A bioassay of a mixture of 1,2,3,6,7,8- and 1,2,3,7,8,9-hexachlorodibenzo-p-dioxin (HCDD) for possible carcinogenicity was conducted by dermal application of a suspension of this substance to Swiss-Webster mice.

Under the conditions of this bioassay, HCDD was not carcinogenic for male or female Swiss-Webster mice.

Single copies of the reports, Biosassay of a Mixture of 1,2,3,6,7,8-Hexachlorodibenzo-p-Dioxin and 1,2,3,7,8,9-Hexachlorodibenzo-p-Dioxin (Gavage) for Possible Carcinogenicity (T.R. 198) and Bioassay of a Mixture of 1,2,3,6,7,8-Hexachlorodibenzo-p-Dioxin and 1,2,3,7,8,9-Hexachlorodibenzo-p-Dioxin (ermal Study) for Possible Carcinogenicity (T.R. 202), are available from the Office of Cancer Communications, National Cancer Institute, Building 31, Room 10A21, National Institutes of Health, Bethesda, Maryland 20205.

Dated: November 14, 1980.

Donald S. Frederickson, M.D.,
Director, National Institutes of Health.

(Catalogue of Federal Domestic Assistance Program Number 13.393, Cancer Cause and Prevention Research. NIH programs are not covered by OMB Circular A–95 because they fit the description of "programs not considered appropriate" in section 8(b) (4) and (5) of that Circular)
[FR Doc. 80–37632 Filed 12–8–80; 8:45 am]
BILLING CODE 4110–08–M

Public Health Service

Health Resources Administration

Application Announcement for Allied Health Professions Traineeship Grants for Advanced Training (Long-Term)

The Bureau of Health Professions, Health Resources Administration, announces that competitive applications for Allied Health Professions Traineeship Grants for Advanced Training (Long-Term) will be accepted under the authority of section 797 of the

Public Health Service Act, as amended.

Section 797 of the Public Health Service Act, as amended, authorizes the Secretary to award grants to public and private nonprofit entities which offer graduate programs to prepare allied health professionals as teachers, administrators, or supervisors.

Eligible entities must offer a degree-granting program at the master's level or higher and meet other specified requirements.

Requests for application materials and questions regarding grant policy should be directed to: Grants Management Officer (A–02), Bureau of Health Professions, Health Resources Administration, Center Building, Room 4–27, 3700 East-West Highway, Hyattsville, Maryland 20782, Telephone: 301–436–7360.

Questions concerning the programmatic aspects of these grants should be directed to: Mr. Charles Munn, Education Development Branch, Division of Associated Health Professions, Bureau of Health Professions, Health Resources Administration, Center Building, Room 5–27, 3700 East-West Highway, Hyattsville, Maryland 20782, Telephone: 301–436–6800.

To be considered for fiscal year 1981 funding, applications must be received by the Grants Management Officer, Bureau of Health Professions at the above address no later than February 6, 1981. Approximately $1,000,000 is expected to be available for these grants.

This program is listed at 13.967 in the Catalog of Federal Domestic Assistance. Applications submitted in response to this announcement are not subject to review by State and areawide clearinghouses under the procedures in the Office of Management and Budget Circular A–95.

Dated: December 4, 1980.

Karen Davis,
Administrator.
[FR Doc. 80–38098 Filed 12–8–80; 8:45 am]
BILLING CODE 4110–83–M

DEPARTMENT OF THE INTERIOR

Heritage Conservation and Recreation Service

National Register of Historic Places; Pending Nominations

Nominations for the following properties being considered for listing in the National Register were received by the Heritage Conservation and Recreation Service before November 28,

Commerce Business Daily

A daily list of U.S. Government procurement invitations, contract awards, subcontracting leads, sales of surplus property and foreign business opportunities

---

U. S. GOVERNMENT PROCUREMENTS

Services

A Experimental, Developmental, Test and Research Work (includes both basic and applied research).

A - - PRIMARY HEALTH CARE: OPERATIONAL RESEARCH. The Agency for International Development is seeking applications for a Cooperative Agreement (CA) to develop and support operational research aimed at closing knowledge gaps impeding efforts to successfully design, implement, and sustain primary health care programs in developing countries. CA staff will be the principal technical resource of this project, and will work collaboratively with AID staff in Washington and the field, host country officials, and researchers from the U.S. and developing countries to: Identify and prioritize issues in country health programs needing study; Mobilize appropriate technical and financial resources to design and conduct studies and disseminate their findings to appropriate audiences. The organizations' principal staff must have substantial technical competence and experience in developing, conducting, managing, and "backstopping" operational research in health in developing countries, appropriate language skills and ability to work with diverse organizational groups. Interested organizations should submit written requests for RFA #AID/DSPE-1029. Telephone requests will not be honored. The issue date will be July 13, 1981. Requests received after COB July 31, 1981 will not be honored. Closing date for submission and acceptance of applications will be August 20, 1981. Furnish two self-addressed, gummed labels. (194)
Department of State, Agency for International Development, Office of Contract Management, Central Operations Division, Room 708-SA-14, Washington, DC 20523

★ **A - - DEVELOP SHIP MODIFICATION TO REDUCE UPTAKE BULKHEAD TEMPERATURE.** Sol. N00167-81-R-0184. Negotiations with Gibbs and Cox, Arlington, VA 22202. See note 46.

★ **A - - RESEARCH TO DETERMINE EFFECTS OF REPAIR WELDING ON FATIGUE OF MARINE GRADE ALUMINUM ALLOY WELDMENTS** (8 ft by 3 ft test specimen) utilizing a fatigue test method development by ALCOA. Negotiations with the ALCOA. Technical Center, ALCOA Center, PA. 15069. See Note 46.

A - - DEVELOPMENT OF INORGANIC SYSTEMS optimized for use as Thermal/Ballistic Armor combining ballistic protection with ambient temperature thermal insulation and incombustibility for ship board use. RFP N00167-81-R-0193 issued approx 20 Jul 80, closing in 20 days. (191)
David W. Taylor Naval Ship R/D Center, Bethesda, MD 20084, Att: G. E. Mayberry, Code 5322, 202/227-1100

A - - ANALYSIS COMPARING SHIPBOARD RAMAN LASER RADAR WITH EXISTING RADIO SONDE SYSTEMS FOR MEASUREMENT OF ATMOSPHERIC PROPERTIES critical to Naval Operations. Analysis shall address accuracy, measurement frequency and location, atmospheric data cloud cover, EMCON/ESM reliability and maintenance design to cost funding and schedule ramifications. RFP N62269-81-r-0822. Closing date on or about 10 August 1981. (191)
Naval Air Development Center (Code 84563), Warminster, PA 18974

★ **A - - INVESTIGATION INTO ZIRCONIUM, TITANIUM AND THEIR ALLOYS** with Molybdenum pressurized to 100 Kilobars at room temperature to study the omega phase transition. Metastable omega phase Crystal structure will be studied by oransition electron microscopy. Ctmwtwtions will be conducted only with Man Labs, Inc., since it is a continuation of work previously performed by a principal investigator. Sol. DAAA22-81-r-0124. Opening date 4 Aug. 81. (194)
Purchasing & Contracting Div., Watervliet Arsenal, Watervliet, NY 12189 518/266-5147

A - - ANALYSIS MF 1980 INSURANCE CLAIMS TO DETERMINE EFFECT OF 1980 BUMPERS ON CRASH DAMAGE. RFP DTNH22-81-R-06013. Evaluate the effectiveness of the Federal Motor Vehicle Safety Standard 215 Bumper Standard for Model Year 1980 passenger cars through collecting and analyzing data on insurance claims. Solicitation mailed to those organizations submitting written requests. see notes 64 and 80. (194)
Dept of Transportation, National hwy Traffic Safety Adm. Office of Contracts and Procurement, 400 Seventh St. SW, Washington, DC 20590

A - - US ARMY'S NEED FOR MOBILITY EQUIPMENT TO SATISFY COMBAT SUPPORT, MINE WAREFARE, AND COMBAT SERVICE SUPPORT FUNCTIONS. The Plan identifies deficiencies in current and projected near term operational capabilities and describes the Science and Technology Base Program applicable to MERADCOM. (191)
US Army Mobility Equipment Research and Development Command, Attn: DRDME-US, Fort Belvoir, VA 22060, Attn: Tim White 703/664-4458

★ **A - - FIRE PROTECTION SYSTEMS DEVELOPMENT**—Anticipate negotiations with Hughes Associates, Inc., Bethesda, MD. See Note 46.

★ **A - - AIRCRAFT GROUND FIRE RISK ANALYSIS AND SUPPRESSION SYSTEM RECOMMENDATIONS**—Anticipate negotiations with Hughes Associates, Inc., Bethesda, MD. See note 46. (191)
Contracting Officer, Naval Research Laboratory, Washington, DC 20375

★ **A - - DEMONSTRATION OF JOSEPHSON JUNCTION SQUID PARAMETRIC AMPLIFIER.** Negotiations with TRW, Inc., Defense & Space Systems Group, Redondo Beach, CA 90278. NRL Synopsis 419. See Note 46. (191)
Contracting Officer Naval Research Laboratory Washington, DC 20375

★ **A - - CRESCENT NOZZLE ANALYSIS** and Performance Projection, RFP DAAH01-81-R-B113 issued o/a 20 Jul 81. Restricted to Science Applications, Inc., 1710 Goodridge Drive, P. O. Box 1303, McLean, VA 22102. See Note 27. (191)
U.S. Army Missile Command, Directorate of Procurement and Production, Redstone Arsenal, AL 35898

★ **A - - PROVIDE RESEARCH ON SURFACE FAULTING** in the Newport-Inglewood Fault Zone. Negotiations conducted with Woodward and Clyde Consultants of Orange, California. See Note 46. (191)
Geological Survey, Procurement and Contracts Section, 345 Middlefield Road, MS-86, Menlo Park, CA 94025

★ **A - - PROCESS FOR HEATLESS PRODUCTION OF HOLLOW FOUNDRY CORES.** Negotiations are being conducted with Anatol Michelson, Sarasota, FL 33579. Sol. DE-FG01-81CS15055 (191)
Dept. of Energy Office of Procurement Operations Washington, DC 20585

H Expert and Consultant Services.

H - - FIRMS SOUGHT TO RECEIVE DRAFT DOCUMENT TITLED "EQUIPMENT AND SOFTWARE REQUIREMENTS FOR FAA COMPUTER-BASED INSTRUCTION SYSTEM," for the purpose of submitting comments on the proposed documents prior to issuing a Request for Proposal for the equipment and software—Based on its experience with an interim computer-based instruction (CBI) system using leased Plato (R) equipment, the FAA has formulated "draft" specifications for complete CBI training center equipment and CBI software—Alternatives to Plato(R) will be considered. The purpose of the CBI program is to reduce the FAA's training costs while improving the quality or effectiveness of training—The scope of the program includes installation of complete CBI training centers at approximately 200 locations in the continental US, Alaska and Hawaii, in the Airway Facilities sectors, Air Route Traffic Control Centers, major Air Traffic Control towers, Flight Inspection field offices, and regional and Washington headquarters. The FAA plans to provide a copy of these draft specifications to interested firms and to solicit their comments on the adequacy of the specifications and other information required by the FAA to finalize program plans for possible future procurement of a CBI system—The draft specifications have been preiously presented to the Interagency Group on Computer-based training and have been endorsed by them as consonant with the Group's standards and goals. (Note: The Government does not intend to award a contract on the basis of this solicitation or otherwise pay for the information solicited—This is not a request for proposal.) The draft specification will be available immediately upon request—Those firms interested in receiving the "Equipment and Software Requirements for FAA Computer-based Instruction System" document should submit a written request on or before 22 Jul 81 to the following address: (190)
FAA Operations Branch, ALG-332 (AJH) 800 Independence Avenue, S.W., Washington, DC 20591

❶ **H - - OPERATION OF OIL ANALYSIS LABORATORY** Hunter Army Airfield, Georgia 31314. IFB DAKF10-81-B-0222. Bid opening date 13 August 1981. (190)
Contracting Division, Bldg. 08 Attn: Ms. Oglesby, Tel (912)767-3360 Fort Stewart, GA 31314

★ **H - - RESEARCH ON POTENTIAL USES OF SPACE.** Negotiations on a selected source basis with Booz-Allen & Hamilton, Inc., Bethesda, MD. See Note 46. (190)
Defense Supply Service-Washington, Room 1D245, The Pentagon, Washington, DC 20310, Attn: T. Bushnell

---

BUSINESS NEWS

LAB INSTRUMENTS EXHIBIT—BRAZIL
The U.S. Department of Commerce will sponsor an exhibition of Scientific-Industrial Laboratory Instruments at the U.S. Trade Center, Sao Paulo, Brazil, Nov. 9-13, 1981. Brazil's scientific-industrial laboratories now play a central role in the country's economic development. Sophisticated instrumentation is manufactured on only a limited basis domestically; therefore, users rely heavily on imports principally from the U.S., West Germany and Japan. U.S. manufacturers who excel in quality, price competitiveness and delivery capability are expected to capture a 35 percent share of the projected total import market of $210 million in 1984. A recent relaxation of tariff barriers makes this the opportune time to exhibit in Brazil. Contact: Gil Terry, Analytical Instruments Project Manager, 202/377-2010.

85 Toiletries.

85 - - RAZOR, SAFETY, Period of contract: June 9, 1981 through April 30, 1982 to Contractor All American Brush Mfg. Company, 37 Empire St., Newark, NJ 07114, Contr. GS-01S-07851, Est. Value $43,987 (BO/TC-M-00264)

General Services Administration, J.W. McCormack Post Office and Courthouse Bldg., Boston, MA 02109

87 Agricultural Supplies.

87 - - FERTILIZER—GS07S06967 & GS07S06968—7CF-52105/T5/7XB—$238,710, Peters Chemical Co., P.O. Box 193, Hawthorne, NJ 07507.

GSA, 819 Taylor St., Fort Worth, TX 76102

91 Fuels, Lubricants, Oils, and Waxes.

91 - - LUBE OIL, DLA600-81-D-1406, 10 Jun. 81—(IFB DLA600-81-0100 and Amendments 1, 2 and 3)—259,590 gallons—$746,326—Bray Oil Co. Inc., 9550 Flair Dr., El Monte, CA.

91 - - LUBE OIL, DLA600-81-D-1404, 10 Jun. 81—(IFB DLA600-81-B-0100 and Amendments 1, 2 and 3)—232,390 gallons—$675,487—Amco Chemical Corp., P.O. Box 208, Oakland, CA

91 - - LUBE OIL, DLA600-81-D-1411, 10 Jun. 81—(IFB DLA600-81-B-0100 and Amendments 1, 2 and 3)—2,640,989 gallons—$6,988,820—Imperial Oil Co. Inc., Orchard Place, P.O. Box G, Morganville, NJ.

91 - - LUBE OIL, DLA600-81-D-1416, 1 Jun 81—(IFB DLA600-81-B-0100 and Amendments 1, 2 and 3)—143,965—$454,219—Southwest Petro-Chem Inc., 1400 S. Harrison, Olathe, KS.

91 - - LUBRICATING OIL, ENGINE, DLA600-81-C-1238 P00001, 8 Jun. 81—(IFB DLA600-81-B-0185 and Amendment 1)—24,750 gallons and 120,000 quarts—$179,654—Delta Petroleum Co., Inc.,P.O. box 10397, Jefferson, LA.

91 - - LUBRICATING OIL, ENGINE, DLA600-81-C-1308, 9 Jun. 81—(IFB DLA600-81-B-0193)—22,000 gallons—$169,950—Delta Petroleum Co. P.O. Box 10397, Jefferson, LA.

91 - - BRAKE FLUID, SILICONE, DLA600-81-C-1293, 5 Jun. 81—(RFP DLA600-81-R-0208) and Amendment 1 and 2—76,800 gallons—$1,118,208—Dow Corning Corp. P.O. Box 1767, Midland, MI.

91 - - DIESEL FUEL MARINE, DLA600-81-D-0297, 28 May 81—(RFP DLA600-81-R-0431)—291,000 gallons—$284,207—Reiss Oil Terminal Corp., 55 Republic Square, Suite 1410, Cleveland, OH.

91 - - COAL BITUMINOUS, DLA600-81-D-1695, 15 Jun. 81—(IFB DLA600-81-B-0214)—16,000 tons—$651,040—R.B.S. Inc., 325 Clark Road, P.O. Box 15352, Cincinnati, OH.

91 - - MOGAS—8,330 gallons; Distillates—1,207,325 gallons, DLA600-81-D-4221, 15 Jun. 81—(IFB DLA600-81-B-0006)—$1,244,105—Knoco Oil Co., P.O. Box 1889, Grand Junction, CO.

91 - - MOGAS—310,000 gallons; Distillages—6,000 gallons, DLA600-81-D-4250 P00001, 11 Jun. 81—(IFB DLA600-81-B-0006)—$372,460—River City Petroleum Inc., P.O. Box 32866, San Antonio, TX.

91 - - LUBRICATING OIL, Aircraft Turbine, DLA600-81-C-1260 P00001, 11 Jun. 81—(IFB DLA600-81-B-0191 and Amendment 1)—220,000 gallons—$550,275—Delta Petroleum Co.Inc., Post Office Box 10397, Jefferson, LA.

91 - - GREASE, MOLYBDENUM DISULFIDE, DLA 600-81-C-1269, 12 Jun. 81—(RFP DLA600-81-R-0381 and Amendment)—1,372 cans and 6,050 cartridges—$48,688—Lubricant Packaging and Supply Co., Inc. 17 Industrial Place, Middletown, NY.

Defense Fuel Supply Center, Cameron Station, Alexandria, VA 22314

91 - - DF-2, DLA600-81-D-0080 P00009, 22 May 81—(RFP DLA600-81-R-0431)—180,000 gallons—$188,820—Enterprise Oil and Gas Co., 14445 Linwood Ave., Detroit, MI.

91 - - HYDRAULIC FLUID, PETROLEUM BASE, DLA600-81-C-1266, 10 Jun. 81—(IFB DLA600-81-B-0100 and Amedments 1, 2 and 3)—90,850 gallons—$443,505—Bray Oil Co., Inc., 9550 Flair Drive, El Monte, CA.

Defense Fuel Supply Center, Alexandria, VA 22314

TRADE LEADS

IMPORTANT NOTICE

Most member countries of the league of Arab States employ a secondary boycott against foreign firms which undertake certain specific types of business relationships with the State of Israel. The Commerce Department will not disseminate nor make available for inspection any tenders or trade opportunity documents which contain conditions intended to support such boycotts, or which are based on documents known to contain such provisions. Trade or investment opportunities published herein are not presently known to be subject to such conditions. However, it is possible that U.S. firms responding to opportunities from Arab countries may be asked at some stage of transaction to participate in an Arab boycott-rela-

ted restrictive trade practice as defined in the department's Export Administration Regulations (15 CFR, Part 369 et seq.)

Firms are reminded that the Export Administration Amendments of 1977 and Export Administration Regulations (16 C.F.R., Part 369) prohibit certain forms of compliance with foreign boycotts, including furnishing information or entering into or implementing agreements. This document or subsequent aspects of this transaction may involve conditions or requirements compliance with which is prohibited. Violators of U.S. anti-boycott law are subject to severe penalties including fine, imprisonment and revocation of export license privilege. Firms are further reminded that any United States person receiving a request for the furnishing of information, the entering into or implementation of agreements, or the taking of any other action which furthers or supports restrictive trade practices or boycott must report such a receipt to the Department of Commerce, in accordance with 15 C.F.R. 396.6.

AGENCY FOR INTERNATIONAL DEVELOPMENT FINANCED

Suppliers of goods and services are advised that the Agency for International Development has a policy of obtaining maximum competiton for projects that it finances. All qualified contractors are encouraged to participate. A.I.D. will not finance any procurement in which boycott or other restrictive trade practices are applied.

THAILAND: AUDIO VISUAL EQUIP., PRINTING MACHINE, COMPUTER - - Group One. Audio visual equipment - slide duplicator, 16mm movie camera, 16mm movie projector, 35mm reflex camera front/rear screen slide projector with tape player. Group Two. Offset printing machine. Group three. Mini Computer CPU, CRT, terminals, printer, floppy disk drive, and software for calculation and analysis of linear programing models, mathematical and statistical package, and scientific sub-routine packages. NOTE: 1. Source/origin other than U.S.A. will be considered in event there is no U.S.A. source. 2. Group 2 and 3 suppliers must have service capability in Bangkok. The purchase will be made under fixed price contracts with payment in U.S. dollars under A.I.D. direct letter of commitment procedures. Documents for submitting bids, including bid procedures, specifications, contracts, and delivery schedules may be obtained by writing Manring Corp., P.O. Box 1865, Bellevue, Washington 98009, Attention AADPC project officer. Include self-addressed stamped (542c) 9x12 envelope. Bid Deadline is 24 August 1981. (194)

SURPLUS PROPERTY SALES

SCRAP: Light and Heavy Steel, Stainless Steel, Paper, Magnetic Tapes, Lead Batteries, Electrical and EElectronic, Copper-Bearing Metal, Copper Wire and Cable, Copper, Cast Iron, Small Arms Cartridge and Shell Cases, Aluminum Wrecked Aircraft, Aluminum. Sealed bid 60-1055 opening 13 Aug. 81. (194)

Defense Property Disposal Reg. Pacific, Box 211, Pearl City, HI 96782, Phone: 808/455-5158

REAL PROPERTY: 0.66 acres improved with a two story brick industrial type bldg; known as the U.S. Army Reserve Center 125-'35 First St., City of Newark, Essex County, NJ. Property is being offered for sale with credit terms available (20% Down, 10 Year Mortgage). Property may be inspected by appointment only. — Sale. GS-02-DRE-11203. Bid opening 19 Aug. 81. (194)

GSA, Federal Property Resources Service, Real Property Div., 26 Fed. Plaza, New York, NY 10278, Tel. 212/264-2625

VESSELS for sale for nontransportation use or for scrapping of the hull in U.S. Category II — Located Beaumont, TX and Portsmouth, VA. Sealed Bid IFB PD-X-1040. Bid opening 13 Aug. 81. (194);

U.S.D.O.C., Maritime Admin. 14th St., Between E & Constitution Ave., N.W. Washington, DC, Attn: J. Fernanders

REAL PROPERTY: - - former Roanoke Rapids Air Force Station, and Housing Area(4-D-NC-582 and 582-A) Roanoke Rapids, North Carolina; 57.29 acres of feland, improved with 27 single family houses, a 14 pad mobile home park, 37 misc. bldgs., roads, streets, structures, facilities and utilities and a 4.28 road easement. IFB 4-D-NC-582 and 582A. Competitive Sealed Bid opening 2 Sep. 81 (194)

General Services Admin. FPRS, Real Property Div., 4DR), Rm. 240, 75 Spring St., SW., Atlanta, GA 30303, Tel. 404/221-5133

Description of Legend

❶ The Procurement item is 100 percent set aside for small business concerns.

❷ A partial quantity or a portion of the procurement item is set aside for small or minority business concerns.

❸ The contract is a labor surplus area set-aside under the provisions of Defense Manpower Policy No. 4B.

❹ Notices of intention to purchase which are published before the IFB's are issued directly to those requesting the proposal.

❺ The procurement will be made in accordance with either DAR part 5, paragraph 2-501 (Military agencies) or FPR part 1-2, paragraph 1, 2.501 (Civil agencies) and is the 1st step of a two step formally advertised procurement. Only those firms submitting qualified responses on the 1st step will receive notifications when the purchase is made.

✭ This synopsis is published for information purposes to alert potential subcontractors and/or suppliers of the proposed procurement. Additional proposals are not solicited.

NUMBERED NOTES are published only on the first working day of each week. The pages containing the "notes" should be retained for reference.

SUBSCRIPTION INFORMATION

$105 a year Priority. $80 Domestic.
6 Month Trial Subscription: $60 Priority $45 Domestic.

To Order. Send remittance with full mailing address to the Superintendent of Documents, Government Printing Office, Washington DC 20402, Tel 202/783-3238 Purchase order must be accompanied by payment. Make checks payable to Superintendent of Documents. Visa or Master Charge also acceptable. Allow approximately 6 weeks for delivery of first issue.

Service Problems. Call Superintendent of Documents Government Printing Office, Washington, DC Tel 202/275-3054.

Expiration. Subscriptions expire one year from the date of the first issue. One expiration notice is mailed about 60 days before expiration date.

Address Changes. Send to Superintendent of Documents, Government Printing Office, Washington, DC 20402, with entire mailing label from last issue received.

EDITORIAL RESPONSIBILITY

The U.S. Department of Commerce (CBD) Room 1304, 433 W. Van Buren St. Chicago, IL 60607, is responsible for compilation and editing only. Tel: 312/353-2950.

U.S. GOVERNMENT PRINTING OFFICE 828-731

The Secretary of Commerce has determined that the publication of this periodical is necessary in the transaction of the public business required by law of this Department. Use of funds for printing this periodical has been approved by the Director of the Office of Management and Budget through 31 Jul 85.

Government Printing Office
Washington DC 20402

Superintendent of Documents
Official Business

SECOND-CLASS MAIL-NEWSPAPER
Postage and Fees Paid
U. S. Government Printing Office
375

FEDERAL FUNDING SOURCES WORKSHEET

LIBRARY PROCEDURE

1. Go to U.S. documents section.
2. Find *Catalogue of Federal Domestic Assistance.*
3. Make key words list.
4. Use subject index and identify your project subject.
5. List programs and their access numbers relevant to your project.
6. Find each program by the access number.
7. Read program description and screen out those least related to your project.
8. Record data from relevant program (on this worksheet).

NOTE: Use the category "related programs" under the program description to identify other potential funding sources. Do steps 6, 7, and 8 until you have researched all relevant programs.

FUNDING AGENCY INFORMATION

Project Name _____

Federal Program _____ CFDA# _____

Federal Agency _____

Address _____

_____

Contact Person _____

Phone _____

Deadline _____

Program Objectives:

Related Programs:

Notes:

Program Priority:

INITIAL PHONE CALL CHECKLIST

For Government and Large Foundations

1. _____ Plan or rehearse your phone call.

2. _____ State your name, title, and organization.

3. _____ "I would like to describe a project we are contemplating and would like to get an assessment of how closely this project fits into your guidelines."

   "Do you have a few minutes to talk?"

   _____ Call Back _____

4. _____ Show that you have done your research. Give reason for your call.

   "I see in the *Federal Register* (or *Foundation Directory*) that you have supported...."

5. _____ "We are planning a...." In 250 words or less describe your project; emphasize the benefits.

6. _____ Ask if the funding source would be interested in supporting such a project or program.

7. _____ Clarify any deviations from guidelines, find out the amount of dollars available nationally and regionally, and determine the current operating *priorities*.

8. _____ If yes, ask to receive grants package and proceed with proposal submission.

   If no, determine why, and find out more about the funding source.

PROPOSAL WRITING PROCESS

Helpful Hints

Short words (5 to 7 letters maximum); avoid jargon.

14- to 17-word sentences with minimal punctuation.

5 to 7 lines per paragraph.

Lots of paragraph headings.

Using of white space and 12-pica type or equivalent; use a word processor where possible.

A sense or urgency, excitement, enthusiasm in proposal.

Use visual aids, charts, pictures.

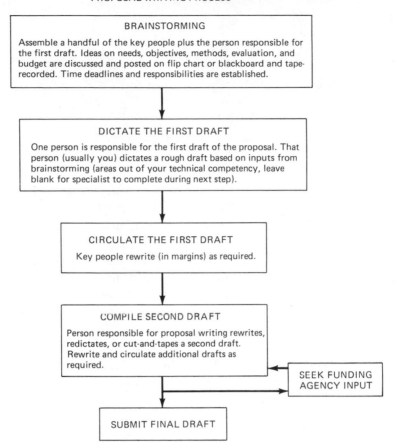

THE TECHNICALLY COMPETENT
PROPOSAL (10 PAGES)

For Government and Large Foundations

TITLE PAGE

Project title, 3 to 5 words, colon, ten maximum

Submitted by: your organization

Submitted to: funding agency

Date of submission

EXECUTIVE SUMMARY (1 PAGE)

Abbreviated: statement of needs, objectives, methods, evaluation, benefits of doing the project, who will be involved, and the budget.

TABLE OF CONTENTS (1 PAGE)
Do this last

INTRODUCTION* (½ TO 1 PAGE)
Purpose of the introduction is to establish your organization's credibility. State your organization's mission, capabilities, and unique features.

NEED STATEMENT (1 TO 2 PAGES)
Your need statement should be factual. For example, avoid broad, generalized statements such as "We in the organization feel...." Instead, use "A survey done by our organization showed ... facts, numbers, percents, and so on." You are attempting to document a problem or need which will be addressed by your organization.

OBJECTIVES, METHODS,* AND EVALUATION (4 TO 6 PAGES)
Each project objective should be derived from one or more identified needs. *Objectives* are the solutions to the needs. They should be written in simple behavioral terms which are easily measurable. Each objective, numbered in turn, should be followed by *methods* (activities) used to achieve that objective. Each specific need will dictate one or more activities. *Evaluation* is the procedure used to measure achievement of the objective.

TIME LINE CHART
The time line is a graphic illustration of the approximate calendar periods to be spent in achieving each project objective. Indicate project milestones (completion of events without which the project cannot proceed). This can sometimes be incorporated into the Grant Management Worksheet.

GRANT MANAGEMENT WORKSHEET (1 PAGE)
This chart has a dual purpose: quick summary information for the proposal reader and management of the project by the project director. Reading across the chart gives a budget for each objective; reading down gives a budget for each category of expense such as personnel, supplies, travel (line item budget).

*Put your dynamite in these sections. They make your proposal unique and fundable.

BUDGET (1 TO 2 PAGES)

A line item budget includes direct costs and indirect costs. The following categories should be included in the *direct cost* part of your line item budget: personnel, fringe benefits, consultants, and contractual services, supplies and services, equipment, travel, and space (space is sometimes considered an indirect cost). If you believe the funding agency might have questions about some unusual or large budget item, include a budget justification. *Indirect costs* are the costs of operating and maintaining the facilities occupied by the project. They are figured as a percent of personnel costs. To establish an indirect cost rate, check with the appropriate government office of management and budget.

FUTURE ACTIVITIES (½ TO 1 PAGE)

List those activities planned (not speculation) which will indicate to the funding agency your organization's long-term commitment to this project.

EXHIBITS

Project administration—how the project will be organized and carried out by your organization. An organization chart showing the relationship of the project to your organization might be helpful. Include documentation such as 501(c)(3) letter.

Support from community, letters of endorsement, news clippings, and so on.

Staff capabilities (vitae).

Other, as required.

OUTLINE YOUR PROPOSAL

TITLE

_____

_____

INTRODUCTION

_____

_____

_____

_____

_____

_____

NEED STATEMENT

_____

_____

_____

_____

_____

_____

_____

_____

_____

THE PROPOSAL CHECKLIST

The data on how government agencies evaluate proposals generally involve the following categories: significance of the problem addressed, quality of the proposed method, competence of staff, agency facilities, adequacy of evaluation, dissemination, budget, and community support. For any given instance there will be other factors influencing the decision to approve or not. These may range from personal interests of reviewers to the old boy's network to political concerns. Government agencies often publish evaluation criteria in the request for proposal (RFP), or you can and should request them before preparing your proposal.

Townsend (1974) found that it was not necessary to have a perfect score on all criteria to get funded. However, you should strive to do your best on each, and by all means, do not rely on just one criterion for success. Lefferts (1980) gives a series of helpful review criteria which he has collected from various organizations. You may want to consider them. The following checklist includes the most important criteria used by govern-

PROJECT MANAGEMENT CHART

OBJECTIVE _____

ACTIVITIES	PERSON(S) RESPONSIBLE	TIME LINE CHART 1 2 3 4 5 6 7 8 9 10 11 12 (months)	PERSONNEL STAFF DAYS¹ COST²	PERSONNEL CONSULTANT DAYS COST	NON-PERSONNEL COSTS SUPPLIES & SERVICES	NON-PERSONNEL COSTS EQUIP-MENT	NON-PERSONNEL COSTS TRAVEL	SPACE³	TOTAL	REMARKS

TOTAL

DONATED

REQUESTED

¹240 days x number of professional staff = total project days
²including salary and fringes
³include here if not charged as indirect cost

Grant management chart.

A. **PERSONNEL:** (Total Salaries and Wages, Fringes, Consultants & Contract Ser.) A.

1. Salaries and Wages

Position	rate/month	X no. mos.	X % time	TOTAL	Requested	Donated
a.						
b.						
c.						
d.						
e.						
f.						
g.						
h.						
i.						
j.						

1.

2. Fringes (SUI, FICA, Workman's Compensation, health insurance, disability, retirement, etc.) 2.

3. Consultants and Contract Services:

	rate/day	X no. days			

3.

Budget worksheet.

B. NON-PERSONNEL COSTS

4. Supplies and Services
   a. Consumable Supplies
   b. Copying
   c. Printing
   d. Computer Costs
   e. Mail
   f. Phone
   g. Insurance
   h. Audit
   i. Subscription
   j.
   k.
   l.

5. Equipment (purchase price or lease rates)
   a.
   b.
   c.
   d.
   e.

6. Travel
   a. Local
   b. Out-of-Town

7. Space (if charged as direct cost)
   a. Rent
   b. Maintenance
   c. Utilities

C. TOTAL DIRECT COST (A - B)

D. TOTAL INDIRECT COSTS

E. TOTAL COSTS (C + D)

Budget worksheet, cont'd

ment agencies in assessing proposals as well as other necessary steps in submitting a fundable proposal.

CHECKLIST

Yes	No	Problem Addressed
___	___	Is the need significant and timely? Is it a community need?
___	___	Does it match the interest of the funding agency?
___	___	Will it have widespread impact?
___	___	Are the results generalizable?

Proposed Method

Yes	No	
___	___	Is it well coordinated and logically laid out?
___	___	Does it answer each identified need?
___	___	Is your method better than most? Is it unique?
___	___	Will the evaluation clearly show one method superior to another?
___	___	Is the budget adequate to carry out the project?

Program Personnel

Yes	No	
___	___	Is the staff experienced and competent in the proposed program area?
___	___	Do they have capability of implementing the project, managing it, and spending the grant money legally?

Grantee Organization

Yes	No	
___	___	Does it have a good track record?
___	___	Does it have adequate facilities?
___	___	Does it have accountability?
___	___	Is there evidence of community support?
___	___	Have you pointed out why your organization should be the one to do the project?

Proposal

Yes	No	
___	___	Is it neatly organized, concise, and well written?
___	___	Is it easy to read and understand?
___	___	Is it ten pages or less, excluding attachments?
___	___	Did you proofread it aloud to a friend?
___	___	Is it packaged correctly, correct number of copies, original on top?
___	___	Was it delivered to the destination by the deadline?
___	___	Was copy of title page sent to congressperson with letter "for your information only"?

__ __ Have you obtained the A-95 review and *all* other sign-offs requested in the guidelines packet?

__ __ Have you included *all* the necessary government forms, filled out completely, and with the proper signatures?

Government forms.

REMOVE AND USE FOR DRAFT COPY

FORM APPROVED
O.M.B. NO. 68-R0249

DEPARTMENT OF HEALTH AND HUMAN SERVICES
PUBLIC HEALTH SERVICE

GRANT APPLICATION

FOLLOW INSTRUCTIONS CAREFULLY

LEAVE BLANK		
TYPE	ACTIVITY	NUMBER
REVIEW GROUP		FORMERLY
COUNCIL/BOARD *(Month, year)*		DATE RECEIVED

1. TITLE OF APPLICATION *(Do not exceed 56 typewriter spaces)*

2. RESPONSE TO SPECIFIC PROGRAM ANNOUNCEMENT ☐ NO ☐ YES *(If "YES," state RFA number and/or announcement title)*

3. PRINCIPAL INVESTIGATOR/PROGRAM DIRECTOR

3a. NAME *(Last, first, middle)*

3b. SOCIAL SECURITY NUMBER

3c. MAILING ADDRESS *(Street, city, state, zip code)*

3d. POSITION TITLE

3e. DEPARTMENT, SERVICE, LABORATORY OR EQUIVALENT

3f. TELEPHONE *(Area code, number and extension)*

3g. MAJOR SUBDIVISION

4. HUMAN SUBJECTS, DERIVED MATERIALS OR DATA INVOLVED
☐ NO ☐ YES *(If "YES," form HHS 596 required)*

5. RECOMBINANT DNA RESEARCH SUBJECT TO NIH GUIDELINES
☐ NO ☐ YES

6. DATES OF ENTIRE PROPOSED PROJECT PERIOD *(This application)*
From: Through:

7. TOTAL DIRECT COSTS REQUESTED FOR PROJECT PERIOD *(from page 5)*
$

8. DIRECT COSTS REQUESTED FOR FIRST 12-MONTH BUDGET PERIOD *(from page 4)*
$

9. PERFORMANCE SITES *(Organizations and addresses)*

10. INVENTIONS *(Competing continuation application only)*
Were any inventions conceived or reduced to practice during the course of the project?
☐ NO ☐ YES - Previously reported
☐ YES - Not previously reported

11. APPLICANT ORGANIZATION *(Name, address, and congressional district)*

12. ORGANIZATIONAL COMPONENT TO RECEIVE CREDIT FOR INSTITUTIONAL GRANT *(See instructions)*
Code ☐ Description:

13. ENTITY IDENTIFICATION NUMBER

14. TYPE OF ORGANIZATION *(See instructions)*
☐ Private Nonprofit
☐ Public *(Specify Federal, State, Local)*:

15. OFFICIAL IN BUSINESS OFFICE TO BE NOTIFIED IF AN AWARD IS MADE *(Name, title, address and telephone number.)*

16. OFFICIAL SIGNING FOR APPLICANT ORGANIZATION *(Name, title, address and telephone number)*

17. PRINCIPAL INVESTIGATOR/PROGRAM DIRECTOR ASSURANCE: I agree to accept responsibility for the scientific conduct of the project and to provide the required progress reports if a grant is awarded as a result of this application.

SIGNATURE OF PERSON NAMED IN 3a *(In ink. "Per" signature not acceptable)*

DATE

18. CERTIFICATION AND ACCEPTANCE: I certify that the statements herein are true and complete to the best of my knowledge, and accept the obligation to comply with Public Health Service terms and conditions if a grant is awarded as the result of this application. A willfully false certification is a criminal offense. (U.S. Code, Title 18, Section 1001.)

SIGNATURE OF PERSON NAMED IN 16 *(In ink. "Per" signature not acceptable)*

DATE

PHS-398
Rev. 5/80

Government forms.

PROTECTION OF HUMAN SUBJECTS
ASSURANCE/CERTIFICATION/DECLARATION

☐ ORIGINAL   ☐ FOLLOWUP   ☐ REVISION

☐ GRANT   ☐ CONTRACT   ☐ FELLOW   ☐ OTHER

☐ NEW   ☐ RENEWAL   ☐ CONTINUATION

APPLICATION IDENTIFICATION NUMBER *(If known)*

STATEMENT OF POLICY: Safeguarding the rights and welfare of subjects at risk in activities supported under grants and contracts from DHHS is primarily the responsibility of the institution which receives or is accountable to DHHS for the funds awarded for the support of the activity. In order to provide for the adequate discharge of this institutional responsibility, it is the policy of DHHS that no activity involving human subjects to be supported by DHHS grants or contracts shall be undertaken unless the Institutional Review Board has reviewed and approved such activity, and the institution has submitted to DHHS a certification of such review and approval, in accordance with the requirements of Public Law 93-348, as implemented by Part 46 of Title 45 of the Code of Federal Regulations, as amended, (45 CFR 46). Administration of the DHHS policy and regulation is the responsibility of the Office for Protection from Research Risks, National Institutes of Health, Bethesda, MD 20205.

1. TITLE OF PROPOSAL OR ACTIVITY

2. PRINCIPAL INVESTIGATOR/ACTIVITY DIRECTOR/FELLOW

3. DECLARATION THAT HUMAN SUBJECTS EITHER WOULD OR WOULD NOT BE INVOLVED

☐ A. NO INDIVIDUALS WHO MIGHT BE CONSIDERED HUMAN SUBJECTS, INCLUDING THOSE FROM WHOM ORGANS, TISSUES, FLUIDS, OR OTHER MATERIALS WOULD BE DERIVED, OR WHO COULD BE IDENTIFIED BY PERSONAL DATA, WOULD BE INVOLVED IN THE PROPOSED ACTIVITY. (IF NO HUMAN SUBJECTS WOULD BE INVOLVED, CHECK THIS BOX AND PROCEED TO ITEM 7. PROPOSALS DETERMINED BY THE AGENCY TO INVOLVE HUMAN SUBJECTS WILL BE RETURNED.)

☐ B. HUMAN SUBJECTS WOULD BE INVOLVED IN THE PROPOSED ACTIVITY AS EITHER: ☐ NONE OF THE FOLLOWING, OR INCLUDING: ☐ MINORS, ☐ FETUSES, ☐ ABORTUSES, ☐ PREGNANT WOMEN, ☐ PRISONERS, ☐ MENTALLY RETARDED, ☐ MENTALLY DISABLED. UNDER SECTION 6. COOPERATING INSTITUTIONS, ON REVERSE OF THIS FORM, GIVE NAME OF INSTITUTION AND NAME AND ADDRESS OF OFFICIAL(S) AUTHORIZING ACCESS TO ANY SUBJECTS IN FACILITIES NOT UNDER DIRECT CONTROL OF THE APPLICANT OR OFFERING INSTITUTION.

4. DECLARATION OF ASSURANCE STATUS/CERTIFICATION OF REVIEW

☐ A. THIS INSTITUTION HAS NOT PREVIOUSLY FILED AN ASSURANCE AND ASSURANCE IMPLEMENTING PROCEDURES FOR THE PROTECTION OF HUMAN SUBJECTS WITH THE DHHS THAT APPLIES TO THIS APPLICATION OR ACTIVITY. ASSURANCE IS HEREBY GIVEN THAT THIS INSTITUTION WILL COMPLY WITH REQUIREMENTS OF *DHHS Regulation 45 CFR 46,* THAT IT HAS ESTABLISHED AN INSTITUTIONAL REVIEW BOARD FOR THE PROTECTION OF HUMAN SUBJECTS AND, WHEN REQUESTED, WILL SUBMIT TO DHHS DOCUMENTATION AND CERTIFICATION OF SUCH REVIEWS AND PROCEDURES AS MAY BE REQUIRED FOR IMPLEMENTATION OF THIS ASSURANCE FOR THE PROPOSED PROJECT OR ACTIVITY.

☐ B. THIS INSTITUTION HAS AN APPROVED GENERAL ASSURANCE (DHHS ASSURANCE NUMBER _____) OR AN ACTIVE SPECIAL ASSURANCE FOR THIS ONGOING ACTIVITY, ON FILE WITH DHHS. THE SIGNER CERTIFIES THAT ALL ACTIVITIES IN THIS APPLICATION PROPOSING TO INVOLVE HUMAN SUBJECTS HAVE BEEN REVIEWED AND APPROVED BY THIS INSTITUTION'S INSTITUTIONAL REVIEW BOARD IN A CONVENED MEETING ON THE DATE OF_____ IN ACCORDANCE WITH THE REQUIREMENTS OF THE *Code of Federal Regulations on Protection of Human Subjects (45 CFR 46).* THIS CERTIFICATION INCLUDES, WHEN APPLICABLE, REQUIREMENTS FOR CERTIFYING FDA STATUS FOR EACH INVESTIGATIONAL NEW DRUG TO BE USED (SEE REVERSE SIDE OF THIS FORM).

THE INSTITUTIONAL REVIEW BOARD HAS DETERMINED, AND THE INSTITUTIONAL OFFICIAL SIGNING BELOW CONCURS THAT:

EITHER ☐ HUMAN SUBJECTS WILL NOT BE AT RISK;   OR ☐ HUMAN SUBJECTS WILL BE AT RISK.

5. AND 6. SEE REVERSE SIDE

7. NAME AND ADDRESS OF INSTITUTION

8. TITLE OF INSTITUTIONAL OFFICIAL | TELEPHONE NUMBER

SIGNATURE OF INSTITUTIONAL OFFICIAL | DATE

HHS-596 (Rev. 5-80)

ENCLOSE THIS FORM WITH THE PROPOSAL OR RETURN IT TO REQUESTING AGENCY.

Government forms.

5. INVESTIGATIONAL NEW DRUGS - ADDITIONAL CERTIFICATION REQUIREMENT

SECTION 46.17 OF TITLE 45 OF THE Code of Federal Regulations states, "Where an organization is required to prepare or to submit a certification . . . and the proposal involves an investigational new drug within the meaning of The Food, Drug, and Cosmetic Act, the drug shall be identified in the certification together with a statement that the 30-day delay required by 21 CFR 130.3(a)(2) has elapsed and the Food and Drug Administration has not, prior to expiration of such 30-day interval, requested that the sponsor continue to withhold or to restrict use of the drug in human subjects; or that the Food and Drug Administration has waived the 30-day delay requirement; provided, however, that in those cases in which the 30-day delay interval has neither expired nor been waived, a statement shall be forwarded to DHHS upon such expiration or upon receipt of a waiver. No certification shall be considered acceptable until such statement has been received."

INVESTIGATIONAL NEW DRUG CERTIFICATION

TO CERTIFY COMPLIANCE WITH FDA REQUIREMENTS FOR PROPOSED USE OF INVESTIGATIONAL NEW DRUGS IN ADDITION TO CERTIFICATION OF INSTITUTIONAL REVIEW BOARD APPROVAL, THE FOLLOWING REPORT FORMAT SHOULD BE USED FOR EACH IND: (ATTACH ADDITIONAL IND CERTIFICATIONS AS NECESSARY).

— IND FORMS FILED: ☐ FDA 1571, ☐ FDA 1572, ☐ FDA 1573

— NAME OF IND AND SPONSOR _____

— DATE OF 30-DAY EXPIRATION OR FDA WAIVER
   (FUTURE DATE REQUIRES FOLLOWUP REPORT TO AGENCY) _____

— FDA RESTRICTION _____

— SIGNATURE OF INVESTIGATOR _____ DATE _____

6. COOPERATING INSTITUTIONS - ADDITIONAL REPORTING REQUIREMENT

SECTION 46.16 OF TITLE 45 OF THE *Code of Federal Regulations* IMPOSES SPECIAL REQUIREMENTS ON THE CONDUCT OF STUDIES OR ACTIVITIES IN WHICH THE GRANTEE OR PRIME CONTRACTOR OBTAINS ACCESS TO ALL OR SOME OF THE SUBJECTS THROUGH COOPERATING INSTITUTIONS NOT UNDER ITS CONTROL. IN ORDER THAT THE DHHS BE FULLY INFORMED, THE FOLLOWING REPORT IS REQUESTED WHEN APPLICABLE.

USE FOLLOWING REPORT FORMAT FOR EACH INSTITUTION OTHER THAN GRANTEE OR CONTRACTING INSTITUTION WITH RESPONSIBILITY FOR HUMAN SUBJECTS PARTICIPATING IN THIS ACTIVITY: (ATTACH ADDITIONAL REPORT SHEETS AS NECESSARY).

INSTITUTIONAL AUTHORIZATION FOR ACCESS TO SUBJECTS

— SUBJECTS: STATUS (WARDS, RESIDENTS, EMPLOYEES, PATIENTS, ETC.) _____
   _____

   NUMBER _____ AGE RANGE _____

   NAME OF OFFICIAL (PLEASE PRINT) _____

   TITLE _____ TELEPHONE _____

   NAME AND ADDRESS OF   _____
   COOPERATING INSTITUTION   _____
                              _____
                              _____

— OFFICIAL SIGNATURE   _____

NOTES: *(e.g., report of modification in proposal as submitted to agency affecting human subjects involvement)*

HHS-596 (Rev. 5-80) (Back)

Government forms.

CHECKLIST

This is the required last page of the application.

Check the appropriate boxes and provide the information requested.

TYPE OF APPLICATION:

☐ NEW application *(This application is being submitted to the PHS for the first time.)*

☐ COMPETING CONTINUATION of grant number: _____ .
(This application is to extend a grant beyond its original project period.)

☐ SUPPLEMENT to grant number: _____ .
(This application is for additional funds during a funded project period.)

☐ REVISION of application number: _____ .
(This application replaces a prior version of a new, competing continuation or supplemental application.)

☐ Change of Principal Investigator/Program Director.
Name of former Principal Investigator/Program Director: _____ .

ASSURANCES IN CONNECTION WITH:

Civil Rights	Handicapped Individuals	Sex Discrimination	Human Subjects General Assurance *(If applicable)*	Laboratory Animals *(If applicable)*
☐ Filed Not filed	☐ Filed Not filed	☐ Filed Not filed	☐ Filed Not filed	☐ Filed Not filed

INDIRECT COSTS:

Indicate the applicant organization's most recent indirect cost rate established with the appropriate DHHS Regional Office. If the applicant organization is in the process of initially developing or renegotiating a rate, or has established a rate with another Federal agency, it should, immediately upon notification that an award will be made, develop a tentative indirect cost rate proposal based on its most recently completed fiscal year in accordance with the principles set forth in the pertinent *DHHS Guide for Establishing Indirect Cost Rates*, and submit it to the appropriate DHHS Regional Office. Indirect costs will not be paid on foreign grants, construction grants, and grants to individuals, and usually not on grants in support of conferences.

☐ DHHS Agreement Dated: _____ .
_____ % Salary and Wages _or_ _____ % Total Direct Costs.

Is this an off-site or other special rate, or is more than one rate involved? ☐ YES ☐ NO
Explanation: _____
_____

☐ DHHS Agreement being negotiated with _____ Regional Office.

☐ No DHHS Agreement, but rate established with _____ Date_____

☐ No Indirect Costs Requested.

Government forms.

POST-PROPOSAL ACTIVITIES

Once you have submitted your proposal, complete and by the deadline, there is nothing else to do but wait. The review cycle is published by the agency and you should abide by it.

The site visit

At your agency: Be hospitable and give the reviewers what they want.

At the state, regional, or Washington office: Take two people. One is preferably a well-informed, articulate board member. Also carry a "heavy briefcase" with materials to back up your request but which were too bulky to submit in the proposal.

What to do if you are

Approved: Thank those involved and your work begins.

Approved but not funded: Find out if and when funding will become available and if and when you must reapply. This may be an opportune time to approach the departmental secretary with your congressperson for discretionary funds, especially if the funding agency staff agree.

Rejected: If your proposal is rejected, you have a responsibility to find out why. You can use the feedback to improve your chances next time. You also have a right to the information and a right to appeal the decision. The latter course should be considered carefully since it will not make you any friends in the funding agency.

FUNDING STRATEGY PORTFOLIO

EXERCISE 1

Make a key words list of three to seven words which describe your project. When in doubt, include the word, since this list will often help you find the obscure funding source. This list can be used to identify corporations and foundations as well.

EXERCISE 2

Identify four potential government funding sources for your project. Indicate the agency name, specific program, contact person, address, phone, type of assistance, funding level, deadlines, agency priorities, operative priorities, and related programs. Remember to record the catalog code number for future reference.

EXERCISE 3
Role play a phone conversation to one of the above funding sources (optional: contact actual agency). *Verify* published priorities, *establish* whether your program qualifies for funding, *determine* current operating priorities, and *ask* for a grants package.

EXERCISE 4
Develop a ten-page technically competent proposal for submission to one of the above agencies. Be sure to include a letter of transmittal with your proposal.

BIBLIOGRAPHY

BARONE, MICHAEL, GRANT UJIFASA, and DOUGLAS MATTHEWS. *Almanac of American Politics.* New York: E. P. Dutton, 1980.

Catalog of Federal Domestic Assistance. Superintendent of Documents, U.S. Government Printing Office, Washington, D.C. 20402. Published annually. The basic tool for federal granting programs. You can find it in most major libraries, or in fellow grantsperson's and congressional representative's offices. Be sure to consult the regular updates.

Circular A-95/What It Is, How It Works. Intergovernmental Division, Office of Management and Budget, Executive Office Building, Washington, D.C. 20503. Also order *A-95 Handbook,* both free.

Commerce Business Daily. Superintendent of Documents, U.S. Government Printing Office, Washington, D.C. 20402. The vehicle for announcement of federal contract opportunities and contract awards over $25,000. Even if you don't contract with the government directly, you might be able to subcontract with the organization or company that does.

Complete Grants Sourcebook For Higher Education. American Council on Education, One Dupont Circle, Washington, D.C. 20036, 1980.

Congressional Directory. Superintendent of Documents, U.S. Government Printing Office, Washington, D.C. 20402.

Congressional Pictorial Directory. Superintendent of Documents, U.S. Government Printing Office, Washington, D.C. 20402.

Congressional Record. Superintendent of Documents, U.S. Government Printing Office, Washington, D.C. 20402.

Consumers Guide to Federal Publications. U.S. Government Printing Office, Washington, D.C. 20402.

Cultural Directory: Guide to Federal Funds and Services for Cultural Activities. Associated Council of the Arts, 1564 Broadway, New York, N.Y. 10036.

DES MARIAS, PHILIP. *How to Get Government Grants.* Public Service Materials Center, 355 Lexington Avenue, New York, N.Y. 10017, 1975.

Directory of Research Grants 1978. Phoenix, Ariz.: Oryx Press, 1981.

ECKSTEIN, BURTON J. *Handicapped Funding Directory.* Research Grant Guides, P.O. Box 357, Oceanside, N.Y. 11572, 1978.

FAUNTLEROY, JAMES, ed. *Federal Education Grants Directory, 1978 Edition.* Capital Publications, 2430 Pennsylvania Avenue, Washington, D.C. 20037. Comprehensive entries on government funding programs in education.

Federal Register. Superintendent of Documents, U.S. Government Printing Office, Washington, D.C. 20402. Daily publication contains detailed information on proposed rules, guidelines, and other important financial information on specific grant programs. Most major libraries subscribe.

Federal Register: What It Is and How To Use It. Superintendent of Documents, U.S. Government Printing Office, Washington, D.C. 20402.

FRIEL, ANN L., ed. *Federal Executive Telephone Directory.* Carroll Publishing Company, 1058 Thomas Jefferson Street, Washington, D.C. 20007.

GABY, PATRICIA V., and DANIEL M. GABY. *Nonprofit Organization Handbook: A Guide to Fund-Raising, Grants, Lobbying, Membership Building, Publicity, and Public Relations.* Englewood Cliffs, N.J.: Prentice-Hall, Inc., 1980.

Grantsmanship Center News. The Grantsmanship Center, 1031 South Grand Avenue, Los Angeles, CA 90015. Bimonthly. A good source of information on government funding, deadlines, and regulations.

Guide to Federal Funds for Urban Programs at Colleges and Universities. American Association of Colleges and Universities, Office of Urban Programs/American Council on Education, Office of Urban Affairs, One Dupont Circle, Washington, D.C. 20036, 1976.

Guide to Institutional Cost Sharing Agreements for Research Grants and Contracts. Office of Administrative Management, Public Health Service, 5600 Fishers Lane, Rockville, Md. 20852. Provides information on setting up a fixed cost-sharing rate for your institution with the federal government.

HALL, MARY. *Developing Skills in Proposal Writing, 2nd Ed.* Continuing Education Publications, 1633 S.W. Park, Portland, Or. 97207, 1978. Good practical guide to writing federal proposals. Contains many sample federal forms.

HILLMAN, HOWARD. *The Art of Winning Government Grants.* New York: Vanguard Press, 1977.

House Directory and *The Senate Directory.* Superintendent of Documents, U.S. Government Printing Office, Washington, D.C. 20402. Contains phone and office number for members and staff.

HUD Newsletter. Superintendent of Documents, Washington, D.C. 20402.

KRATHWOHL, DAVID R. *How to Prepare a Research Proposal.* Syracuse University Bookstore, 303 University Place, Syracuse, N.Y. 13210, 1977. Especially recommended for those seeking funds for behavioral science research.

LEFFERTS, ROBERT. *Getting a Grant: How to Write Successful Grant Proposals.* Englewood Cliffs, N.J.: Prentice-Hall, Inc., 1980.

LRC-W Newsbriefs. Lutheran Resources Commission, Dupont Circle Building, Suite 823, 1346 Connecticut Avenue, N.W., Washington, D.C. 20036. Monthly. Reports on developments in private and public giving and new publications.

Management Circulars A-102, A-110, A-111, 74-4. Publications Office, Office of Management and Budget, 726 Jackson Place, N.W., Washington, D.C. 20006. Free.

Program Planning and Proposal Writing. The Grantsmanship Center, 1031 South Grand Avenue, Los Angeles, Ca. 90015. A good checklist for evaluating the good proposal. Reprint Nos. 100 and 101.

Superintendent of Documents, U.S. Government Printing Office, Washington, D.C. 20402. Order government publications from this address. Include complete identification of item, including the GPO stock number, check or money order, a complete return address, and allow two to three months for delivery. Some items are available at regional GPO bookstores.

TOWNSEND, TED H. "Criteria Grantors Use In Assessing Proposals." *Foundation News* (March/April 1974), pp. 33-38.

United States Government Manual. Superintendent of Documents, U.S. Government Printing Office, Washington, D.C. 20402. Annually. Includes names, addresses, and phone numbers of key government granting agencies.

URGO, LOUIS A. *Manual for Obtaining Government Grants.* Robert J. Corcoran Company, 40 Court Street, Boston, Mass. 02108.

WHITE, VIRGINIA. *Grants: How To Find Out About Them and What To Do Next.* New York: Plenum Press, 1975.

QUIZ

Answer true or false.

1. Government money is easy money.
2. All notices of U.S. government grant programs must first appear in the *Wall Street Journal* before any grant is awarded.
3. RFP is grantsmanship lingo for request for proposal.
4. Block grants are made primarily to neighborhood block organizations.
5. *The Catalogue of Federal Domestic Assistance* is the source book for government funding programs.
6. Your first contact with a government funding agency should be through a well-prepared proposal.
7. If your government grant is "approved but not funded" you may want to approach the Secretary with your congressperson for discretionary funds.
8. Proposal writing is the *most* important aspect of all fund raising.
9. When attending a site visit in the regional office or in Washington, D.C., it is recommended that you take two people and a heavy briefcase.
10. A technically competent proposal to an unsolicited government funding program should not be more than ten pages, excluding attachments.

Answers: (1) F, (2) F, (3) T, (4) F, (5) T, (6) F, (7) T, (8) F, (9) T, (10) T.

Chapter 7

FOUNDATIONS

Foundations are legally incorporated organizations which exist for the sole purpose of giving money away. They make grants in excess of two billion dollars a year to health, education, and social and civic activities. Foundations are perhaps the second most popular source of funds next only to the federal government. Although they give away only about 5 percent of what the government grants, they represent an essential alternative to government funding. The total number of foundations in this country is decreasing.

Before 1969, many foundations were simply tax shelters. Now they are required to give away certain amounts yearly, hold no more than 20 percent stock in any one company, pay a 2 percent excise tax on all gifts made to the foundation, and file annual 990 tax returns with the IRS. The role of the foundation in today's inflated economy becomes one of attempting to maintain steady giving levels with yesterday's endowed dollars. This and the fact that more organizations will be competing for funds to offset shrinking budgets indicate that foundation funds will be scarce in the future.

There are an abundance of resource materials, directories, and books on how to identify foundation giving for your project. The Foundation Funding Sources Worksheet found in this chapter will guide you through them in a systematic way. Locate your nearest Foundation Center Regional Collection. It will have almost everything you need to research thoroughly the foundations of your choice. Begin with the *Foundation Grants Index*. Once you have obtained a list of those foundations which have funded projects like yours, move on to the *Foundation Directory* and the *Source Book Profiles* for detailed information and giving history of the foundation. State foundation directories, where they exist, are proving to be the best single source for identifying the many small, often obscure foundations. When available, obtain a copy of the foundation annual report; otherwise utilize the IRS 990 forms to supplement information on foundation giving. After having gone through this identification procedure, you are ready to prioritize your list of twenty to thirty foundations and begin to contact them by phone.

Foundations must be cultivated very carefully. Foundations through their donors and staffs are "people giving to people." It is very much a process of who knows whom. Interpersonal contacts between your board members and theirs are helpful. Personal contact over the phone and in person is absolutely necessary. Although seemingly innovative in nature, most foundations are very conservative in the projects they fund. No matter how innovative and unique your project is, you must match your interest to theirs. The same rule applies here as with government funding. Do not try to change the foundation's priorities—change yours. This is the primary reason for failure in foundation proposals. Be ready to negotiate your project objectives to match their needs. This is not to say you must compromise your project: just be ready to build a bandshell in order to get the park for your children's recreation program.

Foundation giving culminates in a proposal. With large foundations, this is a ten-page technical proposal. Be aware that 10 percent of foundations have 90 percent of the available staff. With small foundations, there is virtually no one there to read your proposal. Therefore, the proposal to small foundations takes the form of a letter which is usually written to formalize a verbal agreement. This chapter will help you identify and cultivate foundation interests and prepare your proposal.

TYPES OF FOUNDATIONS

DEFINITION OF A FOUNDATION

A foundation is a legally incorporated organization which exists to give money away. The Foundation Center defines a foundation "as a nongovernmental, nonprofit organization, with funds (usually from a single source, either an individual, a family, or a corporation) and program managed by its own trustees or directors, which was established to maintain or aid social, educational, charitable, religious, or other activities serving the common welfare, primarily by making grants to other nonprofit organizations."* Charitable trusts are included.

Excluded are organizations which call themselves "foundations" but whose primary purposes are public fund raising or which aid one institution solely, such as endowments within colleges, churches, hospitals, or the like.

There are other ways of distinguishing between certain types of foundations, for example, by legal form, geographical scope, origin of funds, mode of operation, type of giving, and size of assets or aggregate annual giving. Not all these distinctions are universally accepted, nor does every foundation fit exclusively within a single category. The following are the generally accepted categories of foundations.

INDEPENDENT FAMILY FOUNDATION

The independent family foundation derives its funds usually in the form of an endowment from a wealthy individual or family. Family foundations are categorized as large (over $1 million in assets) or small (under $1 million in assets). There are about 3,000 large foundations and approximately 30,000 small foundations in this country.

CORPORATE FOUNDATION

This type of foundation derives its funds from a proprietary corporation but is operated independently from the corporation for the purposes of making grants. Corporate foundations were established to give stability to a corporation's giving interests apart from the corporation's annual economic fluctuation. Sometimes referred to as "in-and-out" foundations, many corporate foundations do not show large assets but instead show large annual gifts to the foundation by the sponsoring corporation. The corporation and the corporation's foundation often have a coordinated giving policy.

COMMUNITY FOUNDATIONS

Although they share a foundation's charitable purpose, com-

*The Foundation Directory, 8th ed. (New York: The Foundation Center: 1981).

munity foundations are not foundations in the legal sense but are classified by the IRS as tax-exempt, tax-deductible 501(c)(3) organizations. They are not, therefore, private foundations but "public charities" with a community board of directors much the same as schools, churches, hospitals, and certain other nonprofit organizations. They receive funds from many sources rather than one donor or corporation and are not subject to the excise tax or the depletion laws governing foundations. The number of community foundations in this country is increasing.

The Foundation Center defines a fourth category, an *operating foundation*, as a private foundation recognized by the IRS in which the monies are granted exclusively to in-house programs and research.

TWENTY LARGEST INDEPENDENT FOUNDATIONS

Range in asset size: $2.3 billion to $182 million.

Ford Foundation
Johnson (Robert Wood) Foundation
Kellogg (W. K.) Foundation
Mellon (Andrew W.) Foundation
Rockefeller Foundation
Pew Memorial Trust
Kresge Foundation
Lilly Endowment, Inc.
Duke Endowment
Mott (Charles Stewart) Foundation
Carnegie Corporation of New York
MacArthur (John D. and Catherine T.) Foundation
Sloan (Alfred P.) Foundation
Mellon (Richard King) Foundation
Houston Endowment Inc.
Maybee (J. E. and L. E.) Foundation, Inc.
Bush Foundation
Irvine (James) Foundation

Clark (Edna McConnell) Foundation
Rockefeller Brothers Fund

Source: *Foundation Directory*, 7th ed. (New York: The Foundation Center, 1979).

TWENTY LARGEST
COMPANY-SPONSORED FOUNDATIONS

Range in asset size: $3 million to $10 million.

Ford Motor Company Fund
Atlantic Richfield Foundation
Alcoa Foundation
United States Steel Foundation, Inc.
Xerox Fund
Exxon Educational Foundation
Procter & Gamble Fund
Mobil Foundation, Inc.
Minnesota Mining and Manufacturing Foundation, Inc.
Gulf Oil Foundation of Delaware
Eastman Kodak Charitable Trust
Amoco Foundation, Inc.
Dayton Hudson Foundation
Monsanto Fund
General Motors Foundation
General Electric Foundation
General Mills Foundation
Exxon USA Foundation
Shell Companies Foundation, Incorporated
BankAmerica Foundation

Source: *The Foundation Directory*, 7th ed. (New York: The Foundation Center, 1979).

LARGEST COMMUNITY FOUNDATIONS

Range in asset size: $10 million to $212 million.

New York Community Trust
Cleveland Foundation

Chicago Community Trust

Board of Directors of City Trusts, City of Philadelphia

Committee of the Permanent Charity Fund Incorporated

San Francisco Foundation

Hartford Foundation for Public Giving

New Haven Foundation

Kalamazoo Foundation

Columbus Foundation

Philadelphia Foundation

Pittsburgh Foundation

Dallas Community Chest Trust Fund, Inc.

Winston-Salem Foundation

Rhode Island Foundation

California Community Foundation

Indianapolis Foundation

Grand Rapids Foundation

Minneapolis Foundation

Oregon Community Foundation

Source: *The Foundation Directory*, 7th ed. (New York: The Foundation Center, 1979).

SOURCES OF INFORMATION
ON FOUNDATIONS

FOUNDATION CENTER REGIONAL COLLECTIONS

Locate the one nearest you (see the list in this chapter). It will have almost every item referred to in this chapter for your state. Some collections have begun to amass information on other funding sources (government, corporation, etc.) in their Foundation Collection alcove. Also the librarians in charge of these collections are becoming grantspersons in their own right and will assist you in using the materials.

FOUNDATION GRANTS INDEX

Lists grants over $5,000 by large foundations. It is indexed by state, recipients, key words and phrases, and subject category. There is an alphabetical listing of foundations with addresses. It gives the recipient, location, amount given, type and duration of support, and purpose for which the grant was given. The *Index* is updated bimonthly by the *Foundation News*.

Begin with the *Index*; then proceed to other sources for detailed information.

FOUNDATION DIRECTORY

It lists 3,000 largest foundations alphabetically by state and city and by fields of interest. It gives the addresses and phone number, when it was founded, donors, trustees, officers, purpose and activities, assets and grant size, and grant application procedures. Each entry gives a contact person (although this is not always the person you want to contact). There is also an invaluable index of donors, trustees, and administrators which can be useful in cultivating foundations and individual givers.

SOURCE BOOK PROFILES

Each profile provides in-depth updated information on a large foundation. This is probably the best source outside of a personal contact to get to know a foundation's priorities and giving history. Eventually about 1,000 foundations will be listed and regularly updated. You should pay particular attention to this symbol (▼) in the *Foundation Directory*. It indicates that a profile is available on that particular foundation. *Corporate Foundation Profiles* is a separate publication by the Foundation Center.

STATE AND REGIONAL DIRECTORIES

Find out if there is a foundation directory for your state. If so, it will typically contain information similar to that in the *Foundation Directory* but for both large and small foundations. It is the latter information that is so invaluable. An up-to-date listing of state directories is found in this chapter.

NATIONAL DATA BOOK

If you are not fortunate enough to have a foundation directory for your state, then the next best reference is the *National Data Book*. It lists every foundation in the United States by state and city in descending order of asset size. It also lists the foundation's address.

IRS 990S

Filed annually, these IRS forms contain information on how much money and to whom the foundation gave that year. They are a good source of information on smaller foundations which you will find in the *National Data Book* or in your state foundation directory. They are available for foundations in your state at your Regional Collection or by contacting the state attorney general's office.

COMSEARCH PRINTOUTS

The Foundation Center occasionally does an in-depth search of foundation giving by subject and geographic area. These are printed on microfiche and are available through your Regional Collection or may be purchased through the Foundation Center.

OTHER SOURCES

The larger foundations have annual reports which tell you where they have been and where they are going in their funding program and the staff involved.

The catalog entitled *The Grant Seeker's Guide* lists one hundred foundations which fund innovative and change-oriented programs. A copy can be obtained from the National Network of Grantmakers, 919 North Michigan Avenue (fifth floor), Chicago, Illinois 60611 ($7.50pp).

International Philanthropy: available at your Foundation Regional Collection Library.

Foundation Grants to Individuals: available at your Foundation Regional Collection Library.

There are a number of other source books and materials on foundations; many of which will be found in your Foundation Regional Collection.

THE FOUNDATION CENTER

The Foundation Center has a nationwide network of foundation reference collections for free public use. These collections fall within three basic categories. The four reference libraries operated by the Center offer the widest variety of user services and the most comprehensive collections of foundation materials, including all of the Center's publications; books, services and periodicals on foundations and philanthropy; and foundation annual reports, newsletters, and press clippings. The New York and Washington, D.C. libraries contain the IRS returns for all currently active private foundations in the U.S. The Cleveland and San Francisco libraries contain the IRS records for those foundations in the midwestern and western states, respectively. The cooperating collections generally contain IRS records for only those foundations within their state, although they may request information or copies of other records from the New York library.

● This symbol identifies reference collections operated by foundations or area associations of foundations. They are often able to offer special materials or provide extra services, such as seminars or orientations for users, because of their close relationship to the local philanthropic community.

All other collections are operated by cooperating libraries. Generally they are located within public institutions and are open to the public during a longer schedule of hours and also offer visitors access to a well-developed general library research collection.

Please telephone individual libraries for more information about their holdings or hours. To check on new locations call toll free 800–424–9836 for current information.

Where to Go for Information on Foundation Funding

Reference Collections Operated by The Foundation Center

The Foundation Center
888 Seventh Avenue
New York, New York 10106
212–975–1120

The Foundation Center
1001 Connecticut Avenue, NW
Washington, D.C. 20036
202–331–1400

The Foundation Center
Kent H. Smith Library
739 National City Bank Bldg.
629 Euclid
Cleveland, Ohio 44114
216–861–1933

The Foundation Center
312 Sutter Street
San Francisco, Calif. 94108
415–397–0902

Cooperating Collections

ALABAMA
Birmingham Public Library
2020 Park Place
Birmingham 35203
205–254–2541

Auburn University at Montgomery Library
Montgomery 36193
205–279–9110

ALASKA
University of Alaska,
Anchorage Library
3211 Providence Drive
Anchorage 99504
907–263–1848

ARIZONA
Phoenix Public Library
Social Sciences Subject
Department
12 East McDowell Road
Phoenix 85004
602–262–4782

Tucson Public Library
Main Library
200 South Sixth Avenue
Tucson 85701
602–791–4393

ARKANSAS
Westark Community College
Library
Grand Avenue at Waldron Rd.
Fort Smith 72913
501–785–4241

Little Rock Public Library
Reference Department
700 Louisiana Street
Little Rock 72201
501–374–7546

CALIFORNIA
California Community
Foundation
1644 Wilshire Boulevard
Los Angeles 90017
213–413–4042

San Diego Public Library
820 E Street
San Diego 92101
714–236–5816

Santa Barbara Public Library
Reference Section
40 East Anapamu
P. O. Box 1019
Santa Barbara 93102
805–962–7653

COLORADO
Denver Public Library
Sociology Division
1357 Broadway
Denver 80203
303–573–5152

CONNECTICUT
Hartford Public Library
Reference Department
500 Main Street
Hartford 06103
203–525–9121

DELAWARE
Hugh Morris Library
University of Delaware
Newark 19711
302–738–2965

FLORIDA
Jacksonville Public Library
Business, Science, and Industry Department
122 North Ocean Street
Jacksonville 32202
904–633–3926

Miami – Dade Public Library
Florida Collection
One Biscayne Boulevard
Miami 33132
305–579–5001

GEORGIA
Atlanta Public Library
1 Margaret Mitchell Square at
Forsyth and Carnegie Way
Atlanta 30303
404–688–4636

HAWAII
Thomas Hale Hamilton Library
University of Hawaii
Humanities and Social
Sciences Division
2550 The Mall
Honolulu 96822
808–948–7214

IDAHO
Caldwell Public Library
1010 Dearborn Street
Caldwell 83605
208–459–3242

ILLINOIS
● Donors Forum of Chicago
208 South LaSalle Street
Chicago 60604
312–726–4882

Sangamon State University
Library
Shepherd Road
Springfield 62708
217–786–6633

INDIANA
Indianapolis – Marion County
Public Library
40 East St. Clair Street
Indianapolis 46204
317–269–1733

IOWA
Public Library of Des Moines
100 Locust Street
Des Moines 50309
515–283–4259

KANSAS
Topeka Public Library
Adult Services Department
1515 West Tenth Street
Topeka 66604
913–233–2040

KENTUCKY
Louisville Free Public Library
Fourth and York Streets
Louisville 40203
502–584–4154

LOUISIANA
East Baton Rouge Parish Library
Centroplex Library
120 St. Louis Street
Baton Rouge 70802
504–344–5291

New Orleans Public Library
Business and Science Division
219 Loyola Avenue
New Orleans 70140
504–586–4919

MAINE
University of Southern Maine
Center for Research and
Advanced Study
246 Deering Avenue
Portland 04102
207–780–4411

MARYLAND
Enoch Pratt Free Library
Social Science and History
Department
400 Cathedral Street
Baltimore 21201
301–396–5320

MASSACHUSETTS
● Associated Grantmakers of
Massachusetts
294 Washington Street
Suite 501
Boston 02108
617–426–2608

Boston Public Library
Copley Square
Boston 02117
617–536–5400

MICHIGAN
Alpena County Library
211 North First Avenue
Alpena 49707
517–356–6188

Henry Ford Centennial Library
16301 Michigan Avenue
Dearborn 48126
313–943–2337

Purdy Library
Wayne State University
Detroit 48202
313–577–4040

Michigan State University
Libraries
Reference Library
East Lansing 48824
517–353–8816

University of Michigan – Flint
UM – F Library
Reference Department
Flint 48503
313–762–3408

Foundation Center regional collections.

Source: The Foundation Center, 888 Seventh Avenue,
New York, N.Y. 10016.

Grand Rapids Public Library
Sociology and Education Dept.
Library Plaza
Grand Rapids 49502
616–456–4411

Michigan Technological
University Library
Highway U.S. 41
Houghton 49931
906–487–2507

MINNESOTA
Minneapolis Public Library
Sociology Department
300 Nicollet Mall
Minneapolis 55401
612–372–6555

MISSISSIPPI
Jackson Metropolitan Library
301 North State Street
Jackson 39201
601–944–1120

MISSOURI
● Clearinghouse for Mid-
continent Foundations
Univ. of Missouri, Kansas City
Law School, Suite 1–300
52nd Street and Oak
Kansas City 64113
816–276–1176

Kansas City Public Library
311 East 12th Street
Kansas City 64106
816–221–2685

● Metropolitan Association for
Philanthropy, Inc.
5600 Oakland, G-324
St. Louis 63110
314–647–2290

Springfield – Greene County
Library
397 East Central Street
Springfield 65801
417–869–4621

MONTANA
Eastern Montana College
Library
Reference Department
Billings 59101
406–657–2337

NEBRASKA
W. Dale Clark Library
Social Sciences Department
215 South 15th Street
Omaha 68102
402–444–4822

NEVADA
Clark County Library
1401 East Flamingo Road
Las Vegas 89109
702–733–7810

Washoe County Library
301 South Center Street
Reno 89505
702–785–4190

NEW HAMPSHIRE
● The New Hampshire Chari-
table Fund
One South Street
P. O. Box 1335
Concord 03301
603–225–6641

NEW JERSEY
New Jersey State Library
Governmental Reference
185 West State Street
P. O. Box 1898
Trenton 08625
609–292–6220

NEW MEXICO
New Mexico State Library
300 Don Gaspar Street
Santa Fe 87501
505–827–2033

NEW YORK
New York State Library
Cultural Education Center
Humanities Section
Empire State Plaza
Albany 12230
518–474–7645

Buffalo and Erie County Public
Library
Lafayette Square
Buffalo 14203
716–856–7525

Levittown Public Library
Reference Department
One Bluegrass Lane
Levittown 11756
516–731–5728

Plattsburgh Public Library
Reference Department
15 Oak Street
Plattsburgh 12901
518–563–0921

Rochester Public Library
Business and Social Sciences
Division
115 South Avenue
Rochester 14604
716–428–7328

Onondaga County Public
Library
335 Montgomery Street
Syracuse 13202
315–473–4491

NORTH CAROLINA
North Carolina State Library
109 East Jones Street
Raleigh 27611
919–733–3270

● The Winston-Salem Foun-
dation
229 First Union National Bank
Building
Winston-Salem 27101
919–725–2382

NORTH DAKOTA
The Library
North Dakota State University
Fargo 58105
701–237–8876

OHIO
Public Library of Cincinnati
and Hamilton County
Education Department
800 Vine Street
Cincinnati 45202
513–369–6940

Toledo – Lucas County
Public Library
Social Science Department
325 Michigan Street
Toledo 43624
419–255–7055 ext. 221

OKLAHOMA
● Oklahoma City Community
Foundation
1300 North Broadway
Oklahoma City 73103
405–235–5621

Tulsa City-County Library
System
400 Civic Center
Tulsa 74103
918–581–5144

OREGON
Library Association of Portland
Education and Documents Rm.
801 S.W. Tenth Avenue
Portland 97205
503–223–7201

PENNSYLVANIA
The Free Library of Philadelphia
Logan Square
Philadelphia 19103
215–686–5423

Hillman Library
University of Pittsburgh
Pittsburgh 15260
412–624–4528

RHODE ISLAND
Providence Public Library
Reference Department
150 Empire Street
Providence 02903
401–521–7722

SOUTH CAROLINA
South Carolina State Library
Reader Services Department
1500 Senate Street
Columbia 29211
803–758–3181

SOUTH DAKOTA
South Dakota State Library
State Library Building
322 South Fort Street
Pierre 57501
605–773–3131

TENNESSEE
Resources Center for Non-
Profit Agencies, Inc.
502 Gay Street, Suite 201
P. O. Box 1606
Knoxville 37901
615–521–6034

Memphis Public Library
1850 Peabody Avenue
Memphis 38104
901–528–2957

TEXAS
● The Hogg Foundation for
Mental Health
The University of Texas
Austin 78712
512–471–5041

Corpus Christi State
University Library
6300 Ocean Drive
Corpus Christi 78412
512–991–6810

Dallas Public Library
Grants Information Service
1954 Commerce Street
Dallas 75201
214–748–9071 ext. 332

● El Paso Community Foundation
El Paso National Bank Building
Suite 1616
El Paso 79901
915–533–4020

Houston Public Library
Bibliographic & Information
Center
500 McKinney Avenue
Houston 77002
713–224–5441 ext. 265

● Funding Information Library
Minnie Stevens Piper
Foundation
201 North St. Mary's Street
Suite 100
San Antonio 78205
512–227–8119

UTAH
Salt Lake City Public Library
Information and Adult Services
209 East Fifth South
Salt Lake City 84111
801–363–5733

VERMONT
State of Vermont Department
of Libraries
Reference Services Unit
111 State Street
Montpelier 05602
802–828–3261

VIRGINIA
Grants Resources Library
Ninth Floor
Hampton City Hall
Hampton 23669
804–727–6496

Richmond Public Library
Business, Science, & Technology Department
101 East Franklin Street
Richmond 23219
804–780–8223

WASHINGTON
Seattle Public Library
1000 Fourth Avenue
Seattle 98104
206–625 4881

Spokane Public Library
Reference Department
West 906 Main Avenue
Spokane 99201
509–838–3361

WEST VIRGINIA
Kanawha County Public Library
123 Capitol Street
Charleston 25301
304–343–4646

WISCONSIN
Marquette University Memorial
Library
1415 West Wisconsin Avenue
Milwaukee 53233
414–224–1515

WYOMING
Laramie County Community
College Library
1400 East College Drive
Cheyenne 82001
307–634–5853

CANADA
● The Canadian Centre for
Philanthropy
12 Sheppard Street, 3rd Floor
Toronto, Ontario M5H 3A1
416–364–4875

MEXICO
Biblioteca Benjamin Franklin
Londres 16
Mexico City 6, D.F.

PUERTO RICO
Consumer Education and
Service Center
Department of Consumer
Affairs
Minillas Central Government
Building North
Santurce 00904

VIRGIN ISLANDS
College of the Virgin Islands
Library
Saint Thomas
U.S. Virgin Islands 00801
809–774–1252

1/81

Foundation Center regional collections.

Source: The Foundation Center, 888 Seventh Avenue,
New York, N.Y. 10016.

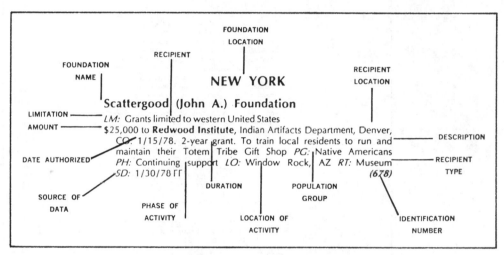

Sample entry from the *Foundation Grants Index*.

Source: *Foundation Grants Index*, The Foundation Center,
888 Seventh Avenue, New York, N.Y. 10016.

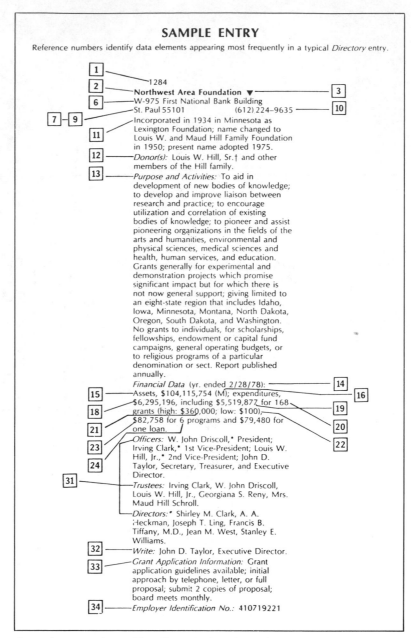

SAMPLE ENTRY

Reference numbers identify data elements appearing most frequently in a typical *Directory* entry.

1 — 1284

2 — **Northwest Area Foundation** ▼ — **3**

6 — W-975 First National Bank Building

7 — **9** — St. Paul 55101   (612) 224-9635 — **10**

11 — Incorporated in 1934 in Minnesota as Lexington Foundation; name changed to Louis W. and Maud Hill Family Foundation in 1950; present name adopted 1975.

12 — *Donor(s):* Louis W. Hill, Sr.† and other members of the Hill family.

13 — *Purpose and Activities:* To aid in development of new bodies of knowledge; to develop and improve liaison between research and practice; to encourage utilization and correlation of existing bodies of knowledge; to pioneer and assist pioneering organizations in the fields of the arts and humanities, environmental and physical sciences, medical sciences and health, human services, and education. Grants generally for experimental and demonstration projects which promise significant impact but for which there is not now general support; giving limited to an eight-state region that includes Idaho, Iowa, Minnesota, Montana, North Dakota, Oregon, South Dakota, and Washington. No grants to individuals, for scholarships, fellowships, endowment or capital fund campaigns, general operating budgets, or to religious programs of a particular denomination or sect. Report published annually.

Financial Data (yr. ended 2/28/78): — **14**

15 — Assets, $104,115,754 (M); expenditures, **16**

18 — $6,295,196, including $5,519,877 for 168 grants (high: $360,000; low: $100), — **19**

21 — $82,758 for 6 programs and $79,480 for one loan. — **20**

23 — *Officers:* W. John Driscoll,* President; Irving Clark,* 1st Vice-President; Louis W. Hill, Jr.,* 2nd Vice-President; John D. Taylor, Secretary, Treasurer, and Executive Director. — **22**

24 —

31 — *Trustees:* Irving Clark, W. John Driscoll, Louis W. Hill, Jr., Georgiana S. Reny, Mrs. Maud Hill Schroll.

Directors: * Shirley M. Clark, A. A. Heckman, Joseph T. Ling, Francis B. Tiffany, M.D., Jean M. West, Stanley E. Williams.

32 — *Write:* John D. Taylor, Executive Director.

33 — *Grant Application Information:* Grant application guidelines available; initial approach by telephone, letter, or full proposal; submit 2 copies of proposal; board meets monthly.

34 — *Employer Identification No.:* 410719221

Sample entry from *The Foundation Directory.*
Source: *The Foundation Directory* (seventh edition), The Foundation Center, 888 Seventh Avenue, New York, N.Y. 10016.

Directory entries are maintained and updated in a computer file. Information in some data fields (8, 35, 36, and 37) does not appear in any printed entry; these data fields are used to generate headings, indices, or statistics. Information in other data fields (3, 4, 5, 23–30) appears only in applicable cases. In some instances applicable data fields in the computer file contain no information because it was not reported.

[1] Entry number. Locator number used in the indices.

[2] Foundation name. The full legal name of the foundation, often transposed to provide proper alphabetical order.

[3] ▼ Identifies foundations for which in-depth descriptions have been prepared for inclusion in *Foundation Center Source Book Profiles* (see Introduction, p. xi).

[4] Former name. Name under which the foundation has previously operated.

[5] Care of (name). Name of an institution or of an individual which should be included in the address to assure delivery of mail.

[6] Street address.

[7] City.

[8] State.

[9] Zip code.

[10] Telephone number. Supplied by the foundation.

[11] Establishment data. Legal form, usually a trust or corporation, and the year and the state in which organized.

[12] Donor name(s). Name(s) of the principal contributor(s) to the foundation, including individuals, families, and/or corporations. If a donor is deceased, the symbol † follows the name.

[13] Purpose and Activities. For the statement of purpose foundations frequently quote Section 501 (c) (3) of the Internal Revenue Code: "...organized and operated exclusively for religious, charitable, scientific, testing for public safety, literary, or educational purposes, or for the prevention of cruelty to children or animals...." When this or similar phrasing is used, it is condensed to read "Broad purposes," or, if "religion" is excluded, "General purposes." In the absence of a clearly defined statement of activities from the foundation, a description is composed on the basis of information appearing on the IRS returns. When the giving is largely confined to the area or state in which the foundation is located, the phrase "primarily local giving"

is applied. If the foundation does not make grants to individuals or, for example, for building or endowment purposes, the statement continues with "No grants to individuals or for building or endowment funds." More detailed restrictions are listed if supplied by the foundation. Finally, if the foundation publishes or issues a report, the paragraph concludes with "Report published [issued] annually" (or "biennially," "every five years," etc.).

[14] Fiscal year date. The year-end date of the foundation's accounting period.

[15] Asset amount. The total value of the foundation's investments. In a few instances, net worth is supplied when the total of mortgages and notes payable and other liabilities exceeds assets by more than ten percent.

[16] Asset type (Market or Ledger value). Generally the asset amount is reported at the market value at the year-end date of the foundation's accounting period.

[17] Gifts received. The amount of new capital received by the foundation in the year of record.

[18] Expenditures. The total disbursements of the foundation, including overhead expenses (salaries, investment, legal, and other professional fees, interest, taxes, rent, and other expenses), federal excise tax, and total grants, matching gifts, scholarships, loans, and/or programs paid.

[19] Grants amount. The total amount of grants paid within the year of record. It does not include commitments for payment in future years.

[20] Number of grants. The number of institutions (or individuals) to which grants were paid.

[21] High grant. The largest typical grant payment.

[22] Low grant. The minimum typical grant payment.

[23] Program amount. In addition to or instead of making grants, some foundations expend funds for internally administered programs.

[24] Number of programs. Some foundations may specify the number of different programs administered internally.

[25] Matching gifts amount. This generally relates to company-sponsored foundations which match employees' gifts, usually to educational institutions.

[26] Number of matching gifts.

[27] Scholarship amount. In addition to or instead of grants, some foundations award scholarships to individuals.

[28] Number of scholarships.

[29] Loan amount. Usually educational loans to students.

[30] Number of loans.

[31] Names and titles of officers and trustees or directors. Some officers may also be trustees and/or directors. When this is the case, an asterisk (*) follows the name of the person.

[32] Write. The name of the person to whom inquiries for information or applications for grants, scholarships, or loans should be addressed.

[33] Grant Application Information. Rules for applying for a grant, month(s) in which the foundation prefers to receive applications, application deadlines, if any, number of copies required, and frequency and dates of board meetings.

[34] Employer Identification No. A number assigned by IRS which is useful in ordering filmed records or paper copies of Forms 990-PF and 990-AR from the Internal Revenue Service.

[35] Fields of interest. Index terms selected from the Purpose and Activities paragraph. See "Index of Fields of Interest."

[36] Limitations. Identifies foundations whose giving is primarily local within the city or state in which they are located. See "Index of Foundations by City and State."

[37] Foundation type. Identifies company-sponsored, operating, or community foundations.

Sample entry from *The Foundation Directory.*
Source: *The Foundation Directory*
(seventh edition),
The Foundation Center,
888 Seventh Avenue, New York, N.Y. 10016.

The Foundation Center
Source Book Profile

Joseph B. Whitehead Foundation

Address:
1400 Peachtree Center Tower
230 Peachtree Street, N.W.
Atlanta, Georgia 30303   **Telephone:** 404-522-6755

Contact: Boisfeuillet Jones, President

Officers:
Boisfeuillet Jones, President
Charles H. McTier, Secretary and Treasurer

Trustees:
J. W. Jones, Chairman
James M. Sibley, Vice-Chairman
Robert W. Woodruff
J. Paul Austin, Alternate Trustee

Financial Data: (Year ended 12/31/79)

Assets (market value):	$ 48,934,557
Gifts Received:	0
Expenditures Including Grants:	$ 2,450,850
Grants Paid:	$ 2,224,500
Number of Grants:	38
High:	$ 750,000
Low:	$ 1,000
General Range:	$10,000-150,000

Background: The Joseph B. Whitehead Foundation was established in 1937 in Georgia by the late Joseph B. Whitehead, Jr., a son of the founder of the Coca-Cola Bottling Company. J. W. Jones, chairman of the foundation's board of trustees, is a vice-president and a director of the Coca-Cola Company, and a director of the Coca-Cola International Corporation. James M. Sibley, vice-chairman, is a senior partner in the Atlanta law firm of King & Spalding. Robert W. Woodruff, trustee, is a director of the Coca-Cola Company.

The officers and trustees of the Joseph B. Whitehead Foundation have the following affiliations with other foundations: Boisfeuillet Jones, president of the Trebor Foundation, the Lettie Pate Evans Foundation, and the Lettie Pate Whitehead Foundation; Charles H. McTier, secretary of the Trebor Foundation, and secretary-treasurer of both the Lettie Pate Evans Foundation and the Lettie Pate Whitehead Foundation; J. W. Jones, chairman of both the Trebor Foundation and the Lettie Pate Evans Foundation; James M. Sibley, vice-chairman of the Trebor Foundation, a trustee of the Lettie Pate Evans Foundation and a member of the distribution committee of the Marian W. Ottley Trust-Atlanta; and Robert W. Woodruff, a donor of the Trebor Foundation and a trustee of the Lettie Pate Evans Foundation. The foundation's staff consists of six part-time members.

Foundation Publications: None

Purpose: Grants limited to the local area, primarily for education, youth programs and child welfare, care of the aged, the arts, and civic affairs.

Grant Analysis

The foundation's level of giving has fluctuated over the past few years, from $1.57 million in 1977, to $2.26 million in 1978, to $2.22 million in 1979. In 1979, as in previous years, the foundation's grants were disbursed to a wide variety of Atlanta organizations. The main portion of funding (34%) was awarded in a single grant of $750,000 to the United

© The Foundation Center 1981

Source: The Foundation Center, 888 Seventh Avenue, New York, N.Y. 10016.

Way of Metropolitan Atlanta, Inc. Grants for health and medical education accounted for 30% of funds. The main recipient in this category was the Shepherd Spinal Center ($300,000). Major support was also awarded to the Henrietta Egleston Hospital for Children (two grants totaling $215,000) and Emory University (four grants totaling $137,000). A variety of youth and child welfare organizations received 24% of the grant monies, with significant funding awarded to the Metropolitan Atlanta Boys' Clubs, Inc. and Junior Achievement of Greater Atlanta, Inc. ($150,000 each). The balance of funding was disbursed to an arts alliance and a botanical garden (6%); social welfare agencies (4%); conservation organizations (1%); and two secondary schools (1%). Five of the grantees in 1979 were first-time recipients.

	No. of grants	Amount	Percent of grant dollars
Community Fund	1	$ 750,000	34
Health Care/Hospitals	9	677,500	30
Youth/Child Welfare	16	525,000	24
Cultural Programs	2	125,000	6
Social Welfare	6	82,000	4
Conservation	2	35,000	1
Secondary Education	2	30,000	1
	38	$2,224,500	100%

Types of Support: In general, support for building funds, equipment and materials, land acquisition, renovation projects, and general purposes. Limited support for scholarships. The foundation generally refrains from giving grants for endowments, research-related programs, or matching gifts. No loans. The foundation awards single-year grants only.

In 1979, support for building and development funds, capital improvements, scholarships, studies, a demonstration project, equipment and supplies, camperships, the purchase of buildings and property, and general support.

Recipient Type: In 1979, recipients included the United Way of Metropolitan Atlanta, Inc.; hospitals, a spinal center, a school of medicine, and a school of dentistry; two youth development agencies and various child welfare agencies, including orphanages, day care centers, and nurseries; an arts alliance and a botanical garden; social welfare organizations, including urban and regional programs, a safety council, and a counseling center; conservation associations; and secondary schools. No grants to individuals.

Geographic Distribution: Grants are limited to Atlanta, Georgia. In 1979, one recipient was located in Decatur, Georgia.

Grants: The following is a complete list of grants paid by the foundation in 1979. Recipients are located in Atlanta, Georgia unless otherwise indicated.

Community Fund

United Way of Metropolitan Atlanta, Inc. $750,000
    For purchase of adjacent property for development

Whi

Source: The Foundation Center, 888 Seventh Avenue,
New York, N.Y. 10016.

Health Care/Hospitals

Shepherd Spinal Center	$300,000
For new facility	
Henrietta Egleston Hospital for Children	215,000
Hospital expansion, $200,000	
Care of indigent patients, $15,000	
Emory University	137,500
For improved computerized head and body scanner to be located at Grady Memorial Hospital, $97,500	
School of Dentistry, for scholarships, $15,000	
School of Medicine, for scholarships, $15,000	
Emory University Hospital, for care of indigent patients, $10,000	
Saint Joseph's Hospital of Atlanta, Inc.	15,000
Care of indigent patients	
Society of St. Vincent de Paul, Particular Council of Atlanta	10,000
Care of the indigent	

Youth/Child Welfare

Junior Achievement of Greater Atlanta, Inc.	150,000
To construct an economic education center and administrative office in North Fulton County	
Metropolitan Atlanta Boys' Clubs, Inc.	150,000
General operation support, $90,000	
Capital improvements and repair of buildings, $60,000	
Council for Children, Inc.	55,000
For two-year volunteer foster care review demonstration project in cooperation with the Fulton County Department of Family and Children's Services	
Bedford-Pine Day Care Center, Inc.	50,000
To construct a child and family resource center to be located in the Bedford-Pine Urban Renewal Area	
Child Service and Family Counseling Center	22,000
Scholarship support for needy children, $20,000	
Christmas gifts for needy children, $2,000	
Carrie Steele-Pitts Home, Inc.	15,000
Building repairs and improvements, additions, equipment, and Christmas gifts for children	
Gate City Day Nursery Association	15,000
Building repairs and improvements, equipment, and Christmas gifts for needy children	
Georgia Baptist Children's Home, Inc.	15,000
Building repairs and improvements, equipment, and Christmas gifts for children	
Sheltering Arms Association of Day Nurseries	15,000
Equipment and supplies, and Christmas gifts for children	
The United Methodist Children's Home, Decatur, GA	15,000
Building repairs and improvements, equipment, and Christmas gifts for children	
Hillside Cottages	10,000
Building repairs, improvements, equipment, and Christmas gifts for children	

Source: The Foundation Center, 888 Seventh Avenue, New York, N.Y. 10016.

Southern Christian Home	$ 10,000
Building repairs, improvements, equipment, and Christmas gifts for children	
Fulton County Department of Family and Children's Services	2,000
Christmas gifts for needy children	
Jewish Children's Service	1,000
For summer camperships	

Cultural Programs

Atlanta Arts Alliance	100,000
Contingent fund for planning and development	
The Atlanta Botanical Garden	25,000
Toward implementation of three-year development plan	

Social Welfare

Capacity, Inc.	50,000
Support of Urban Design Team	
Georgia Association of Pastoral Care, Inc.	15,000
General support of pastoral counseling program	
Atlanta Regional Commission	10,000
Alliance for Human Services Planning Study, $5,000	
Study proposal for the Assessment of Special Service Needs among the Hispanic Population of the Atlanta Area, $5,000	
Georgia Safety Council	5,000
General support of educational programs	
Southeastern Council of Foundations	2,000
General support	

Conservation

Outdoor Activity Center, Inc.	25,000
Purchase of the Hartnett School building for use as part of nature center in West End area of Atlanta	
The Georgia Conservancy	10,000
General support of public education programs	

Secondary Education

Saint Francis Day School	15,000
Building repairs and alterations at private school for children with special learning disabilities	
The Schenck School, Inc.	15,000
Building repairs and alterations at private school for children with special learning disabilities	

Policies, Guidelines, and Application Procedures: The foundation prefers that initial contact or inquiry be made by letter, followed by one copy of the full proposal. Although the foundation specifies no application deadline, it prefers to receive proposals in January or September. The board meets semiannually in April and November. Receipt of proposals is acknowledged. The foundation will grant an interview at the request of the applicant, but preferably only when the proposal is determined to be of program interest. The applicant should expect to wait no more than one year before receiving notification of final action on a proposal, though an average time has not been determined. The foundation does not issue grant application guidelines or require completion of an application form.

Sources: 990-AR, 990-PF, Information supplied by the foundation.

3/81
fv

Source: The Foundation Center, 888 Seventh Avenue, New York, N.Y. 10016.

STATE FOUNDATION DIRECTORIES

STATE	TITLE	PREPARED BY	ADDRESS	COST
Alabama	Guide to Foundations of the Southeast, Vol. IV (out of print)	Davis-Taylor Assoc., Inc.	Davis-Taylor Assoc., Inc. Route 3, Box 289 Williamsburg, Ky. 40769	$25.00
	Foundation Philanthropy in the Southeast (covers 11 states)	Charles S. Rooks	Southeastern Council of Foundations 134 Peach St. Atlanta, Ga. 30303	$4.00 pp.
Arkansas	Included in A Guide to Foundations of the Southeast, Vol. IV (out of print)	Davis-Taylor Assoc., Inc.	(See Alabama)	
California	Where the Money's At	Patricia Blair Tobey and Irvin R. Warner	ICPR Publications 9255 Sunset Blvd., 8th Floor, Los Angeles, Cal. 90069	$19.00 pp.
	Guide to California Foundations (1981 edition)	Melinda Marble	Guide 210 Post St. #814 San Francisco, Cal. 94108	$6.00 pp.
	Registry of Charitable Trusts		Wells Fargo Bank Building 5th Street and Capital Mall Room 443 Sacramento, Cal.	$5.50
	Small Change from Big Bucks: Bay Area Foundations	Herb Allen and Sam Sternberg	Bay Area Committee for Responsive Philanthropy 944 Market St. San Francisco, Cal. 94102	$6.00 pp.
	The San Diego County Foundation Directory		Community Congress of San Diego 1172 Morena Blvd. San Diego, Calif. 92110	$10.00
Colorado	Colorado Foundation Directory	Junior League of Denver, Denver Foundation and Attorney General of Colorado	Junior League of Denver, Inc. 1805 Bellaire, Suite 400 Denver, Col. 80222	$7.00 pp.
Connecticut	Directory of Foundations in state of Connecticut	John Parker Huber	Eastern Connecticut State College Foundation Box 431 Willmantic, Conn. 06226	$7.00 pp.
	Connecticut Foundation Directory	Michael E. Burns	Develop & Technical Asst. (DATA) State St. New Haven, Conn. 06511	$10.00

State	Title	Author/Compiler	Address	Price
Delaware	*Delaware Foundations*	United Way Planning Committee Project for Agency Consultation and Training	Jeanna Dougherty, Planning Associate United Way of Del., Inc. 701 Shipley St. Wilmington, Del. 19801	$ 7.50 pp.
D.C.	*The Washington D.C. Metropolitan Area Foundation Directory*	Julia Mills Jacobsen and Kay Carter Courtade	Management Communications Publications Division 4416 Edmunds St., N.W. Washington, D.C. 20007	$13.50
Florida	*Guide to Foundations in Florida*	Susan M. Cook	Department of Community Affairs 2571 Executive Center Circle E. Tallahassee, Fla. 32301	$4.50
Georgia	*Georgia Foundation Directory*	Ann Bush	Atlanta Public Library 10 Pryor Street, S.W. Atlanta, Ga. 30303	—
Hawaii	*A Guide to Charitable Trusts and Foundations in the State of Hawaii*	Alu Like	Alu Like 2828 Paa St., Suite 3035 Honolulu, Hi. 96819	$10.00
Idaho	*Directory of Idaho Foundations*	Caldwell Public Library	Caldwell Public Library 1010 Dearborn St. Caldwell, Ida. 83605	$1.00 pp.
Illinois	*Illinois Foundation Directory*	B. J. Capriotti and F. J. Capriotti, III	Foundation Data Center 100 Wesley, Temple Building 123 E. Grant St. Minneapolis, Minn. 55403	$425.00
Indiana	*Indiana Foundation Directory*	Paula Reading Spear	Central Research Systems 320 N. Meridian, Suite 1011 Indianapolis, Ind. 46204	$19.95 pp.
Kansas	*Directory of Kansas Foundations*	Connie Townsley	Assoc. of Community Arts Councils of Kansas Columbian Building, 4th Floor 112 W. 6th Topeka, Kans. 66603	$5.80 pp.
Kentucky	*A Guide to Foundations of the Southeast, Vol. I (out of print)*	Davis-Taylor Assoc., Inc.	(See Alabama)	
Louisiana	*A Guide to Foundations of the Southeast, Vol. IV (out of print)*	Davis-Taylor Assoc., Inc.	(See Alabama)	
Maine	*A Directory of Foundations in the State of Maine, 2nd ed.*	Foundation Regional Collection Librarian	University of Southern Maine Center for Research and Advanced Study 246 Deering Ave. Portland, Me. 04102	$3.50 pp.

State	Title	Source	Address	Price
Maryland	1977 Annual Index Foundation Reports		Office of the Attorney General 1 South Calvert St. Baltimore, Md. 21202 (See Connecticut)	$5.00 pp.
Massachusetts	Directory of Foundations in the Commonwealth of Massachusetts, 2nd ed.	John Parker Huber		$15.00 pp.
	Community Grants Resource Catalogue	Steve Rubin and Don Levitan	Government Research Publications Box 122 Newton Centre, Mass. 02159	$9.00
	Directory of Foundations in Massachusetts	Attorney General and Association of Foundations of Greater Boston	University of Massachusetts Press Box 429 Amherst, Mass. 01002	$7.50 pp.
Michigan	Michigan Foundation Directory, 3rd ed.	Council of Michigan Foundations, Michigan League for Human Services	Michigan League for Human Services 200 Mill St. Lansing, Mich. 48933	$9.00 pp.
Minnesota	Guide to Minnesota Foundations	Minnesota Council on Foundations	Minnesota Council on Foundations Suite 413, Foshay Tower 9th & Marquette Avenues Minneapolis, Minn. 55402	$10.00
Mississippi	Included in a Guide to Foundations of the Southeast, Vol. IV (out of print)	Davis-Taylor Assoc., Inc.	(See Alabama)	
Montana	Directory of Montana and Wyoming Foundations	Eastern Montana College Foundation	Eastern Montana College Foundation 1500 North 30th St. Billings, Mont. 45901	$ 5.00 pp.
Nebraska	Nebraska Foundation Directory	Junior League of Omaha	Junior League of Omaha 7365 Pacific St. Omaha, Neb. 68114	
New Hampshire	A Directory of Foundations in the State of New Hampshire	John Parker Huber	(See Connecticut)	$5.00 pp.
	Directory of Charitable Funds in New Hampshire		Office of the Attorney General State House Annex Concord, New Hampshire 03301	$2.00

State	Title	Author/Publisher	Address	Price
New Jersey	1979 Supplement, $1 1980 Supplement, $? *The Mitchell Guide to New Jersey Foundations, Corporations and Their Managers*	Janet Mitchell, publisher	Mitchell Guides Box 413 Princeton, N.J. 08540	$20.90
	Foundations in New Jersey		Governmental Reference Office New Jersey State Library Box 1898 Trenton, N.J. 08625	
New York	*New York Foundation Profiles*	Davis-Taylor Assoc., Inc.	(See Alabama)	$29.95
	The Mitchell Guide to New York Foundations, Corporations, and Their Managers, Vols. I, II, III	Janet Mitchell, publisher	Mitchell Guides Box 413 Princeton, N.J. 08540	$25.00 pp. (each)
North Carolina	*A Guide to Foundations of the Southeast, Vol. II* (out of print)	Davis-Taylor Assoc., Inc.	(See Alabama)	
Ohio	*Charitable Foundations Directory of Ohio*		Office of the Attorney General 30 East Broad St. 15th Floor Columbus, Ohio 43215	$5.00 pp.
	A Guide for Charitable Foundations in the Greater Akron Area	CETA Workers and United Way	Human Services Planning Library United Way of Summit County P.O. Box 1260 90 N. Prospect St. Akron, Ohio 44309	$2.50
Oklahoma	*Directory of Oklahoma Foundations*	Thomas E. Broce	University of Oklahoma Press 1005 Asp Ave. Norman, Okla. 73069	$9.95
Oregon	*Directory of Foundations, and Charitable Trusts Registered in Oregon*	Virgil D. Mills	Dept. of Justice 500 Pacific Bldg. 520 S.W. Yamhill Portland, Ore. 97204	$5.00
	Guide to Oregon Foundations	Tri-County Community Council	Tri-County Community Council 718 Burnside, Portland, Ore. 97209	$8.00 pp.
Pennsylvania	*Directory of Charitable Organizations—1976*		Office of the Attorney General Capital Annex Harrisburg, Pa. 17120	$10.50
	Directory of Pennsylvania Foundations	S. Damon Kletzien Margaret H. Chalfant Frances C. Ritchey	Free Library of Philadelphia Logan Square at 19th St. Philadelphia, Pa. 19103	$14.00 pp.
	Pittsburgh Area Foundation Directory		Community Action Pittsburgh, Inc. Planning & Research Division Fulton Bldg., 107 6th St. Pittsburgh, Pa. 15222	$10.00

State	Title	Compiler/Publisher	Address	Price
	The Metropolitan Philadelphia Philanthropy Study		Regional Science Dept. University of Pennsylvania Philadelphia, Pa. 19104	$8.00
Rhode Island	*A Directory of Foundations in the State of Rhode Island*	John Parker Huber	(See Connecticut)	$5.00 pp.
South Carolina	*South Carolina Foundation Directory*	Anne K. Middleton	South Carolina State Library P.O. Box 11469 Columbia, S.C. 29211	$.70
Tennessee	*A Guide to Foundations of the Southeast, Vol. I. (out of print)*	Davis-Taylor Assoc., Inc.	(See Alabama)	
Texas	*Directory of Texas Foundations*	Wm. J. Hooper	Texas Foundations Research Center P.O. Box 5494 Austin, Tex. 78763	$19.85 pp.
	The Guide to Texas Foundations		Dallas Public Library Publishing Services 1954 Commerce St. Dallas, Tex. 75201	$10.00 pp.
Vermont	*A Directory of Foundations in the State of Vermont*	Denise M. McGovern	Eastern Connecticut State College Foundation Box 431 Willmantic, Conn. 06226	$3.00 pp.
Virginia	*Virginia Directory of Private Foundations*	Office of Human Resources	Dept. of Intergovernmental Affairs 4th St., Office Bldg. Richmond, Va. 23219	$2.00 pp.
Washington	*Charitable Trust Directory*	Attorney General	Office of Attorney General Temple of Justice Olympia, Wash. 98504	$3.00 pp.
West Virginia	*West Virginia Foundation Directory*	William Secto	West Virginia Foundation Directory Box 96, Route #1 Terra Alta, W.V. 26764	$7.95 pp.
Wisconsin	*Foundations in Wisconsin: A Directory 1980*	Barbara Szyszko Friedman and Margaret Marik	Foundation Collection Marquette University Memorial Library 1415 W. Wisconsin Ave. Milwaukee, Wisc. 53233	$12.50 pp.

*Where no directory exists, check the attorney general's office for copies of the IRS 990 forms on foundations in that state. Use the Foundation Center's *National Data Book* as a guide.

THE FOUNDATION CENTER

How to Find the Information You Need on an Aperture Card

Forms 990-PF and 990-AR are the information returns which private foundations are required to file each year with the Internal Revenue Service. Form 990-PF provides fiscal details on receipts and expenditures, compensation of officers, capital gains or losses, and other financial matters. Form 990-AR provides information on foundation managers, assets, grants paid and/or committed for future payment. The IRS films these two forms and makes them available on aperture cards. An aperture card is a conventional tabulator card which contains a window in which film is mounted. You may view aperture cards at The Foundation Center's main libraries or national and regional collections. You may also order aperture cards by state or on individual foundations from the IRS.

Each foundation has at least two aperture cards. Many have more cards depending on the number of special attachments to the return. The film part of the aperture card contains up to 14 pages. The basic pages of Forms 990-PF and 990-AR are always filmed in the same sequence and will be found in the same location on each card. The 990-PF and 990-AR are each filmed on a separate card from left to right in three consecutive rows.

Below is a reproduction of the aperture card.

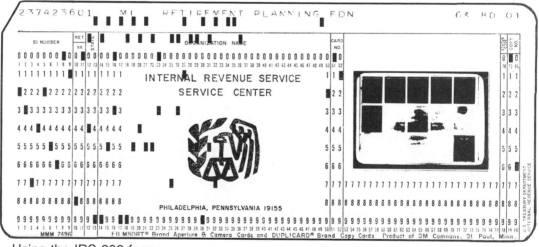

Using the IRS 990 forms.
Source: The Foundation Center, 888 Seventh Avenue, New York, N.Y. 10016.

ORDER FORM (Check desired subjects)

COMSEARCH: SUBJECTS

Order Number/Title	Number of Records

Communications
- ☐ 1. Film, Documentaries, Media & Audio-visuals — 267
- ☐ 2. Television, Radio & Communications — 304
- ☐ 3. Journalism, Publishing & Literature — 416

Education
- ☐ 16. Public Primary & Secondary Education — 321
- ☐ 17. Independent Primary & Secondary Ed — 522
- ☐ 18. Higher Ed — Buildings & Equipment — 446
- ☐ 19. Higher Ed — General Support — 366
- ☐ 20. Higher Ed — Special projects — 575
- ☐ 21. Higher Ed — Scholarships — 549
- ☐ 22. Higher Ed — Fellowships — 292
- ☐ 23. Libraries — 532
- ☐ 24. Educational Research — 220
- ☐ 25. Vocational Counseling, Career & Adult Education — 405
- ☐ 26. Educational Associations — 325
- ☐ 27. Educational Administration & Personnel Development — 188
- ☐ 28. Higher Ed — Loans & Other Student Aid — 204

Health
- ☐ 31. Medical Education — 328
- ☐ 32. Medical Research — 358
- ☐ 33. Dentistry & Nursing — 207
- ☐ 34. Hospitals — Buildings & Equipment — 345
- ☐ 35. Hospitals — Programs — 483
- ☐ 36. Medical Care & Rehabilitation — 504
- ☐ 37. Mental Health — 404
- ☐ 38. Public Health — 247
- ☐ 39. Alcoholism & Drug Abuse — 140

Humanities
- ☐ 46. Art & Architecture — 422
- ☐ 47. Theater & Performing Arts — 568
- ☐ 48. Music — 530
- ☐ 49. Museums — 459
- ☐ 50. Historical Projects — 269
- ☐ 51. Dance — 180

Population Groups
- ☐ 61. Aged — 356
- ☐ 62. Handicapped — 473
- ☐ 63. Women — 537
- ☐ 64. Minorities — General — 345
- ☐ 65. Blacks — 444
- ☐ 66. Native Americans, Hispanics & Orientals — 319

Physical & Life Science
- ☐ 75. Biology & Nutrition — 236
- ☐ 76. Agriculture — 275
- ☐ 77. Chemistry, Physics & Math — 367
- ☐ 78. Environmental Programs — 558
- ☐ 79. Computer Technology & General Tech — 180

- ☐ 80. Energy — 163
- ☐ 81. Engineering — 276

Social Studies
- ☐ 85. Business — 350
- ☐ 86. Economics — 278
- ☐ 87. Government & Political Science — 274
- ☐ 88. Legal Programs & Law Schools — 589
- ☐ 89. Psychology & Sociology — 309

Welfare
- ☐ 91. Public Interest, Citizen Participation & Consumerism — 321
- ☐ 92. Urban Development, Housing & Trans — 561
- ☐ 93. Community Funds — 553
- ☐ 94. Crime & Delinquency — 266
- ☐ 95. Social Agencies — 504
- ☐ 96. Family Services & Population Studies — 540
- ☐ 97. Child Welfare — 554
- ☐ 98. Young Men's & Women's Associations — 284
- ☐ 99. Boys and Girls Scouts & Clubs — 317
- ☐ 100. Youth Programs — 393
- ☐ 101. Animal Welfare — 120
- ☐ 102. Rural Development — 154
- ☐ 103. Recreation & Athletics — 317
- ☐ 104. Camps — 196

Other
- ☐ 105. International — Domestic Recipients — 641
- ☐ 106. International — Foreign Recipients — 639
- ☐ 107. Religion — Welfare & Theology — 555
- ☐ 108. Matching & Challenge Grants — 351
- ☐ 109. Conferences & Seminars — 377

COMSEARCH: GEOGRAPHIC

Order Number/Title	Number of Records
☐ 261. New York City	2788
☐ 260. Washington, D.C.	1053
☐ 205. California	2011
☐ 213. Illinois	976
☐ 221. Massachusetts	905
☐ 222. Michigan	774
☐ 223. Minnesota	754
☐ 230. New Jersey	611
☐ 232. New York State (except New York City)	626
☐ 235. Ohio	664
☐ 238. Pennsylvania	1489
☐ 243. Texas	1263

Subject & Geographic Sample

```
Accession number
             1741407
             Scattergood (John A.) Foundation, NY —————— Foundation name and location
Amount ——— $25,000 to Redwood Institution, Indian Artifacts Department,— Recipient name and location
             Denver, CO. To rebuild museum shop at Totem Tribe Reservation. —
Date authorized —1/2/79                                                    Description
             YRS. DURATION: 2
Recipient contact— PROFILE: Museum, American Indians, Matching grant, Chinle, AZ. —— Site of activity
             LIMITATION: Grants not usually made for building programs
Source of data — REFERENCE: John B. Cummings, Director                     Type of support
             SOURCE: 1/8/79 FF
Subject code — C: 3.6  MC: HUMANITIES, SC: MUSEUMS,                         Target population
             KEY WORDS: Museum, American Indian/Indian (American) museum

             Recipient type   Main category   Sub-category
```

Hundreds of grant records like this make up each *Subject & Geographic COMSEARCH*. For each printout we retrieve related grants of $5000 or more from our own Foundation Grants Computer Data Base. In 1979 over 19,000 grants to nonprofit organizations were reported by over 400 foundations, including all of the top 100 foundations.

COMSEARCH: SPECIAL TOPICS

Order Number/Title	Number of Records
☐ 301. Largest Foundations by Asset Size	1000
☐ 302. Largest Foundations by Grant Size	1000
☐ 303. Largest Company-Sponsored Foundations	600
☐ 304. Operating Foundations	1417

Special Topics Sample

THE FOUNDATIONS DATABANK
Thousand Largest Foundations by Assets

SEQ NO.	FOUNDATION NAME	ST CD	ASSET AMOUNT	TOTAL GIVING	GRANTS AMOUNT	NO. OF GRANTS	FISCAL DATE
1	Ford Foundation, The	NY	2,291,480,000	146,905,570.00	132,310,570	1,998	9/30/78
2	Johnson (The Robert Wood) Foundation	NJ	863,062,049	44,775,631.00	44,775,631	344	12/31/78
3	Kellogg (W. K.) Foundation	MI	792,274,191	43,679,426.00	43,679,426	498	8/31/79
4	Mellon (The Andrew W.) Foundation	NY	776,376,006	40,698,688.00	40,698,688	183	12/31/77
5	Rockefeller Foundation, The	NY	739,889,103	43,601,243.00	31,718,053	610	12/31/77
6	Pew Memorial Trust, The	PA	604,988,351	35,890,700.00	35,890,700	297	12/31/78
7	Kresge Foundation, The	MI	586,902,197	25,269,100.00	25,269,100	215	12/31/78
8	Lilly Endowment, Inc.	IN	524,345,394	31,725,935.00	31,725,935	306	12/31/77
9	Duke Endowment, The	NC	423,492,195	24,840,157.00	24,840,157		12/31/77
10	Mott (Charles Stewart) Foundation	MI	396,876,032	28,453,117.00	28,453,117	366	12/31/78

COMSEARCH printouts.

Source: The Foundation Center, 888 Seventh Avenue, New York, N.Y. 10016.

FOUNDATION FUNDING SOURCES WORKSHEET

Grants Index Information

Your Project Name _____

LIBRARY PROCEDURE

1. Locate foundation collection.
2. Locate the *Foundation Grants Index.*
3. Make key words list describing your project.
4. Search the Subject Index and Common Words Index using *key words.*
5. Copy down the access numbers for the most appropriate index entries.
6. Locate funding agencies by using the access numbers. Pay particular attention to those access numbers corresponding to your state.
7. Read entry and screen out those least related to your program.
8. Record data from *Grants Index* on this worksheet.

FOUNDATION INFORMATION

Funding information from *Grants Index* and other sources. Use additional sheets as needed.

1. Foundation Name * ☐☐☐☐☐☐
   Funded Project Title _____
   Grantee Organization _____
   _____
   Size of Grant __ Access Number __

2. Foundation Name * ☐☐☐☐☐☐
   Funded Project Title _____
   Grantee Organization _____
   _____
   Size of Grant __ Access Number __

3. Foundation Name * ☐☐☐☐☐☐
   Funded Project Title _____
   Grantee Organization _____
   _____
   Size of Grant __ Access Number __

5. Foundation Name * ☐☐☐☐☐☐
   Funded Project Title _____
   Grantee Organization _____
   _____
   Size of Grant __ Access Number __

9. Go to the *Foundation Directory* and record additional data on page 2 of this worksheet.

10. Go to *Source Book Profiles* and foundation annual reports for more detailed information.

11. Go to your state foundation directory.

12. Go to the IRS 990 forms.

Foundation Directory Information*

Project Name _____

Foundation Name _____

Address _____

_____

Contact Person _____

Title _____ Phone _____

Principal Actors (donors, trustees, etc.)

Funding History

*Fill out one of these sheets for each separate foundation using information from *Foundation Directory*, *Source Book*, 990s, and annual reports.

_____
_____
_____
_____

Funding Priorities

_____
_____
_____
_____
_____

Comments

_____
_____
_____
_____
_____

THE INITIAL PHONE CALL

For Foundations or Corporations

1. _____ Plan or rehearse your phone call (purpose of the phone call is to get you into a meeting with the chief decision maker).

2. _____ State your name, title, and organization.

3. _____ Show you have done your research.
"I see that your foundation (corporation) has been (is) involved in programs for...."

4. _____ Give reason for your call.
"We are planning a...."
"Do you have a few minutes to talk?"
If no, "When can I call back?"

5. _____ In 250 words or less, paint the benefits of your project (be sure to include *quid pro quo*).

6. _____ Ask the funding source if they might be interested in supporting a project which provides these benefits.

If yes, set up a meeting and end the conversation immediately.

If no, find out why and determine more about the funding source and obtain at least one referral.

PROPOSAL WRITING PROCESS

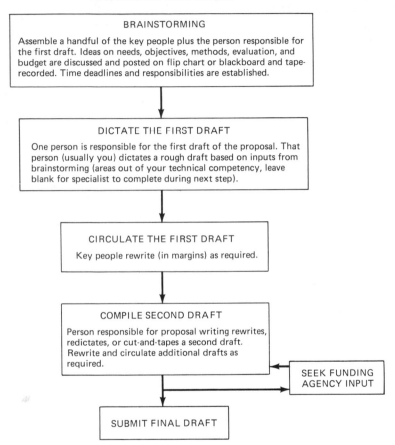

PROPOSAL WRITING PROCESS

HELPFUL HINTS

Short words (5 to 7 letters maximum); avoid jargon.

14- to 17-word sentences with minimal punctuation.

5 to 7 lines per paragraph.

Lots of paragraph headings.

Use of white space and 12-pica type or equivalent; use a word processor where possible.

A sense of urgency, excitement, enthusiasm in proposal.
Use visual aids, charts, pictures.

THE TECHNICALLY COMPETENT PROPOSAL (10 PAGES)

For Government and Large Foundations

TITLE PAGE
Project title, 3 to 5 words, colon, ten maximum
Submitted by: your organization
Submitted to: funding agency
Date of submission

EXECUTIVE SUMMARY (1 PAGE)
Abbreviated: statement of needs, objectives, methods, evaluation, benefits of doing the project, who will be involved, and budget.

TABLE OF CONTENTS (1 PAGE)
Do this last.

INTRODUCTION* (½ TO 1 PAGE)
Purpose of the introduction is to establish your organization's credibility. State your organization's mission, its capabilities, and unique features.

NEED STATEMENT (1 TO 2 PAGES)
Your need statement should be factual. For example, avoid broad, generalized statements such as "We in the organization feel...." Instead, use "A survey done by our organization showed ... facts, numbers, percents, and so on." You are attempting to document a problem or need which will be addressed by your organization.

OBJECTIVES, METHODS,* AND EVALUATION (4 TO 6 PAGES)
Each project objective should be derived from one or more identified needs. *Objectives* are the solutions to the needs. They should be written in simple behavioral terms which are easily

*Put your dynamite in these sections. They make your proposal unique and fundable.

measurable. Each objective, numbered in turn, should be followed by *methods* (activities) used to achieve that objective.
Each specific need will dictate one or more activities. *Evaluation*
is the procedure used to measure achievement of the objective.

TIME LINE CHART

The time line is a graphic illustration of the approximate calendar periods to be spent in achieving each project objective.
Indicate project milestones (completion of events without which
the project cannot proceed). This can sometimes be incorporated
into the Grant Management Worksheet.

GRANT MANAGEMENT WORKSHEET (1 PAGE)

This chart has a dual purpose: quick summary information for
the proposal reader and management of the project by the project
director. Reading across the chart gives a budget for each objective; reading down gives a budget for each category of expense
such as personnel, supplies, travel, and so on (line item budget).

BUDGET (1 TO 2 PAGES)

A line item budget includes direct costs and indirect costs. The
following categories should be included in the *direct cost* part of
your line item budget: personnel, fringe benefits, consultants,
and contractual services, supplies and services, equipment,
travel, and space (space is sometimes considered an indirect
cost). If you believe the funding agency might have questions
about some unusual or large budget item, include a budget
justification. *Indirect costs* are the costs of operating and maintaining the facilities occupied by the project. They are figured as
a percentage of personnel costs. To establish an indirect cost rate,
check with the appropriate government office of management
and budget.

FUTURE ACTIVITIES (½ TO 1 PAGE)

List those activities planned (not speculation) which will indicate to the funding agency your organization's long-term
commitment to this project.

EXHIBITS

Project administration—how the project will be organized and
carried out by your organization. An organization chart showing

the relationship of the project to your organization might be helpful. Include documentation such as 501(c)(3) letter.

Support from community, letters of endorsement, news clippings, and so on.

Staff capabilities (vitae).

Other, as required.

OUTLINE YOUR PROPOSAL

TITLE

INTRODUCTION

NEED STATEMENT

LETTER PROPOSAL
TO SMALL FOUNDATIONS

Introductory statement.

Objectives of your proposal.

Description of your program and its operations.

What your program will do for the community.

Particular relevance to the foundation's interests.

Budget: salaries, materials, services.

Attachments: brochures, news clippings, 501(c)(3) letter, and possibly a recent auditor's report.

NOTE: Keep it under six pages including attachments.

FUNDING STRATEGY PORTFOLIO

EXERCISE 1

Identify six foundations appropriate to your project: two large, two small family foundations, one corporate foundation, and one community foundation. Give name and address and describe the funding priorities, past giving history, and principal actors involved (e.g., trustees). Be sure to include pertinent information on projects similar to yours which were recently funded by the foundation. Who would you initially contact from each of the named foundations, and what is his or her position or role?

EXERCISE 2

Role play a telephone conversation with the decision maker in a small family foundation in your area (optional: contact actual person). Who is the person you will be speaking to? *Verify* the foundation's published priorities, *establish* whether your program qualifies for funding, *determine* any current emphases in priorities, and *arrange* for a meeting.

EXERCISE 3

Write a proposal suitable for presentation to one of the foundations you have selected.

PROJECT MANAGEMENT CHART

OBJECTIVE _____

ACTIVITIES	PERSON(S) RESPONSIBLE	TIME LINE CHART 1 2 3 4 5 6 7 8 9 10 11 12 (months)	PERSONNEL STAFF DAYS[1]	COST[2]	CONSULTANT DAYS	COST	NON-PERSONNEL COSTS SUPPLIES & SERVICES	EQUIP-MENT	TRAVEL	SPACE[3]	TOTAL	REMARKS
											TOTAL	
											DONATED	
											REQUESTED	

[1] 240 days x number of professional staff = total project days

[2] including salary and fringes

[3] include here if not charged as indirect cost

Budget worksheet.

BUDGET EXERCISE

A. PERSONNEL: (Total Salaries and Wages, Fringes, Consultants & Contract Ser.)				TOTAL	Requested	Donated
1. Salaries and Wages			A.			
Position	rate/month	X no. mos.	X % time			
a.						
b.						
c.						
d.						
e.						
f.						
g.						
h.						
i.						
j.						
2. Fringes (SUI, FICA, Workman's Compensation, health insurance, disabil- ity, retirement, etc.)			2.			
3. Consultants and Contract Services:			3.			
	rate/day	X no. days				

Grant management chart.

Grant management chart, cont'd

B.	NON-PERSONNEL COSTS		
4.	Supplies and Services		
	a. Consumable Supplies		
	b. Copying		
	c. Printing		
	d. Computer Costs		
	e. Mail		
	f. Phone		
	g. Insurance		
	h. Audit		
	i. Subscription		
	j.		
	k.		
	l.		
5.	Equipment (purchase price or lease rates)		
	a.		
	b.		
	c.		
	d.		
	e.		
6.	Travel		
	a. Local		
	b. Out-of-Town		
7.	Space (if charged as direct cost)		
	a. Rent		
	b. Maintenance		
	c. Utilities		
C.	TOTAL DIRECT COST (A + B)		
D.	TOTAL INDIRECT COSTS		
E.	TOTAL COSTS (C + D)		

Remarks:

St. Catherine Community Hospital

3OOO ARBOR LAKE DRIVE
LANSING, MICHIGAN 489O4
(517)-387-7673

January 15, 1981

Russell Gamber, President
The Gamber Foundation
One North Plaza
Lansing, Michigan   48810

Dear Mr. Gamber:

St. Catherine Community Hospital is a 750-bed acute care facility
serving the residents of Lansing, Michigan and the surrounding
rural areas and small communities. St. Catherine opened in 1934
with sixty beds to serve the needs of Lansing's growing population.

Due to the unique proportions of industrial and agricultural activity
in southwestern Michigan, Lansing has an above average incidence
of physical handicaps due to injury. The Hospital has grown consid-
erably since its opening and is now one of the leaders in the
treatment of the physically handicapped. St. Catherine believes
that a patient's physical and psychological needs must receive
consideration in the development and implementation of treatment.

A 1976 study revealed that St. Catherine's patients in physical
and occupational therapy had a higher rate of rehospitalization
than the national average. Action was taken to determine ways
of lowering the rate to the national average or below. A two
year trial program of horticulture therapy proved the effect-
tiveness of such a program to meet the psychological needs of
the physically impaired.

Your past giving record has proven your support of credible
institutions offering innovative programs to the handicapped. We
are planning to implement a complete horticulture therapy
program into our rehabilitation unit. This requires an on-site
barrier free greenhouse, a van with wheelchair lift, a full-time
horticulture therapist and two support personnel. The greenhouse
will serve as a non-institutional setting for the motivation
and interest of patients. Because of Lansing's agricultural history,
the greenhouse will also serve as an acclimation center between
the hospital and the community for the disabled patient.

158

The total cost of completing the project is #394,039. We are requesting $321,249 to construct and equip the greenhouse. Groundbreaking has been planned for April of 1982 with a completion date of November 1982.

I look forward to meeting with you at your convenience to discuss the proposal and provide further information.

Sincerely yours,

Karen L. Findlay

Karen L. Findlay
Director of Development
St. Catherine Community Hospital

Sample letter proposal.

Source: *Michigan Foundation Directory* (second edition), Michigan League for Human Services, 200 Mill Street, Lansing, MI 48933.

FOUNDATION ASSESSMENT OF PROPOSALS

Criteria foundations use in assessing proposals vary, but include many of the following considerations.

1. Competence of persons involved
   a. Quality of project staff (Are they among the best of all possible people to undertake the venture?)
2. Feasibility of the proposal
   a. Is the time right for the endeavor?
   b. Is the action proposed adequate to solve the problem addressed?
   c. Is the sponsoring agency or institution clearly enthusiastic about the substance of the proposal?
   d. Are the proposed facilities and staffing sufficient for the job?
3. Importance and utility of the venture to the community or to society
   a. Is there a demonstrable need for the project?
   b. Whom will the project benefit and how?
   c. Is it based on ethical and moral premises?
   d. Will there be a measurable improvement if the venture is successful? Will harm be done if it fails?
4. Originality and creativity of the proposed venture
   a. Does the project duplicate or overlap other existing or past programs?
   b. Is it new and innovative? Alternatively, does it help conserve beneficial programs that might otherwise atrophy or be lost?
   c. Could the project be carried out better elsewhere or by other persons?
5. Appropriateness of the project to the foundation's policy and program focus
   a. Is the program consonant with the foundation's program objectives?
   b. If so, does it address an area that should receive priority in consideration of proposals?
6. Prospects for leverage and pattern-making effects
   a. Will the project draw in other financial support (if needed)?
   b. Will the project produce significant changes?
   c. Will the results be transferable to other projects and localities?
7. Need for foundation support
   a. Are public sources of funds available (Federal, state, and local governments)?
   b. Are other private sources more appropriate (other foundations more active in the field, other private institutions or individuals)?
8. Soundness of the budget
   a. Is it adequate for the job to be accomplished, but not so generous as to be wasteful?
   b. Is it evident that the project director (or principal support staff) is familiar with the administrative intricacies of conducting the proposed project — and that he has planned carefully for contingencies?
9. Persistence, dedication and commitment of the proposers
   a. Have they persevered in efforts to secure needed funds?
   b. Have they devoted sufficient time to planning and launching the venture?
   c. Is the project one of their primary interests or a major professional preoccupation?
10. Provision of objective evaluation of results, where feasible
    a. Will the project staff maintain adequate records to demonstrate success of the project?
    b. Where the project lends itself to statistical evaluation, has provision been made for recording and analyzing relevent data?
    c. Where necessary, has appropriate evaluation advice been sought?

Foundations are looking for creative uses for their resources. If you have a project that really merits foundation support, promote it!

BIBLIOGRAPHY

ALLEN, HERB, ed. *The Bread Game: The Realities of Foundation Fund-Raising,* 2nd ed. San Francisco: Glide Publications, 1974.

Annual Register of Grant Support, 1980-81. Chicago: Marquis Academic Media, 1980.

Annual reports. The foundations' annual reports usually include the most current and accurate data available on giving. Call or write the foundation.

"Community Foundations: The Wave of the Future." *The Grantsmanship Center,* 1031 South Grand Avenue, Los Angeles, CA 90015. Reprint No. 304.

Complete Grants Source Book for Higher Education. American Council on Education, One Dupont Circle, Washington, D.C. 20036, 1980.

Corporate Foundation Profiles: Complete Analyses of the Largest Company-Sponsored Foundations. Foundation Center, 888 Seventh Avenue, New York, N.Y. 10016, 1980.

DERMER, JOSEPH. *How to Get Your Fair Share of Foundation Grants.* Public Service Materials Center, 355 Lexington Avenue, New York, N.Y. 10017, 1973.

————.*How to Write Successful Foundation Presentations.* Public Service Materials Center, 355 Lexington Avenue, New York, N.Y., 10017, 1975.

DERMER, JOSEPH, ed. *Where America's Large Foundations Make Their Grants.* Public Service Materials Center, 355 Lexington Avenue, New York, N.Y. 10017, 1980.

ECKSTEIN, BURTON J., ed. *Handicapped Funding Directory, 1978-79.* Research Grants Guides, P.O. Box 357, Oceanside, N.Y. 11572, 1978.

Foundation Annual Reports: What They Are and How to Use Them. Foundation Center, 888 Seventh Avenue, New York, N.Y. 10016. Includes addresses of foundations that publish annual reports.

Foundation Center Comsearch Printouts. Foundation Center, 888 Seventh Avenue, New York, N.Y. 10016. Available in print or microfiche.

Foundation Center National Data Book. Foundation Center, 888 Seventh Avenue, New York, N.Y. 10016. Vols. I and II.

Foundation Center Source Book Profiles. Foundation Center, 888 Seventh Avenue, New York, N.Y. 10016.

Foundation Directory. Foundation Center, 888 Seventh Avenue, New York, N.Y. 10016. Every two years.

Foundation Grants Index. Irvington, N.Y.: Columbia University Press. Annually in April.

Foundation Grants to Individuals, 2nd edition. Foundation Center, 888 Seventh Avenue, New York, N.Y. 10016, 1979.

Foundation News. Foundation News, P.O. Box 783, Chelsea Station, New York, N.Y. 10011, bimonthly. This publication updates the *Foundation Grants Index* as well as having excellent articles.

Foundation Report/Foundation Reporter Supplement/News Monitor on Philanthropy/Hot Line News. Taft Products, Inc., 1000 Vermont Avenue, N.W., Washington, D.C. 20005.

The Future of Foundations: Some Reconsiderations. Change Magazine Press, NBW Tower, New Rochelle, N.Y. 10801, 1978.

Giving in America: Toward a Stronger Voluntary Sector. Commission on Private Philanthropy and Public Needs, 1776 K Street, Washington, D.C. 20001, 1975.

Grants and Awards Available to American Writers, 10th ed. P.E.N. American Center, New York, N.Y., 1978.

HILLMAN, HOWARD. *The Art of Winning Foundation Grants.* New York: Vanguard Press, 1975.

How to Apply to a Foundation. Citizen's Energy Project, 6th Street, N.W., Suite 300, Washington, D.C. 20001, 1980.

IRS 990-AR and 990-PF returns. All private foundations are required to file these returns, which include valuable lists of trustees and grants. Available in the Foundation Center Regional Collections.

JACQUETTE, F. LEE, and BARBARA L. JACQUETTE. *What Makes a Good Proposal?* Foundation Center, 888 Seventh Avenue, New York, N.Y. 10016, 1977.

KURZIG, CAROL. *Foundation Fundamentals: A Guide for Grant Seekers.* Foundation Center, 888 Seventh Avenue, New York, N.Y. 10016, 1980.

LRC-W Newsbriefs. Lutheran Resources Commission, Dupont Circle Building, Suite 823, 1346 Connecticut Avenue, N.W., Washington, D.C. 20036. Monthly.

MARGOLIN, JUDITH B. *About Foundations: How to Find the Facts You Need to Get a Grant,* rev. ed. Foundation Center, 888 Seventh Avenue, New York, N.Y. 10016, 1977.

MARTINSON, JEAN ANN. *International Philanthropy: A Compilation of Grants by U.S. Foundations.* Foundation Center, 888 Seventh Avenue, New York, N.Y. 10016, 1978.

MAYER, ROBERT A. *What Will a Foundation Look For When You Submit a Grant Proposal?* Foundation Center, 888 Seventh Avenue, New York, N.Y. 10016, 1977.

NASON, JOHN W. *Trustees and the Future of Foundations.* Hoke Communications, Inc., 224 7th Street, Garden City, N.Y. 11530, 1977.

National Directory of Arts Support by Private Foundations. Washington International Arts Letter, Box 9005, Washington, D.C. 20003, 1979.

Philanthropic Digest. Brakeley, John Price Jones, Inc., 1100 17th Street, Suite 912, N.W., Washington, D.C. 20036. Sixteen issues per year.

RICHARDS, MARILYN W. *Funding Resources for Women in Development Projects.* Secretariat for Women in Development, New TransCentury Foundation, 1789 Columbia Road, N.W., Washington, D.C. 20009, 1979.

Robin Hood Was Right: A Guide to Giving Money for Social Change. Vanguard Public Foundation, 4111 24th Street, San Francisco, Cal. 94114, 1977.

SHELLOW, JILL R., ed. *The Grant Seeker's Guide.* The National Network of Grantmakers, 919 North Michigan Avenue (fifth floor), Chicago, Ill., 60611, 1981.

State foundation directories. This chapter contains a list of available state directories. They vary in quality, but often contain valuable information on smaller foundations not found in the *Foundation Directory.* Your state's foundation directory is a *must.*

STRUCKHOFF, EUGENE C. *Handbook for Community Foundations.* Council on Foundations, P.O. Box 783, Old Chelsea Station, New York, N.Y. 10011, 1977.

Trustees of Wealth: The Taft Guide to Philanthropic Decision Makers. Taft Products, Inc., 1000 Vermont Avenue, Washington, D.C. 20005, yearly.

U.S. Foundations and Minority Group Interests. U.S. Human Resources Corporation, San Francisco, Cal., 1975.

WILSON, WILLIAM K., ed. *Directory of Research Grants.* Phoenix, Ariz.: Oryx Press, 1980.

Foundations Outside the United States

AUSTRALIA. *Directory of Philanthropic Trusts in Australia.* Australian Council for Educational Research, Federick Street, Hawthorn, Victoria: 3122, Australia, 1968. 226 listings, 274 pages.

CANADA. *Canadian Universities' Guide to Foundations and Granting Agencies,* 3rd ed. Information Division of the Association of Universities and Colleges of Canada, 151 Slater, Ottawa KIP, Canada, 1973. 300 listings, 161 pages. This directory includes U.S. foundations that support Canadian institutions.

EUROPE. *Guide to European Foundations.* Prepared by the Giovanni Agnelli Foundation. Irvington, N.Y.: Columbia University Press, 1973. 296 listings, 401 pages.

FRANCE. *Foundations.* Published under the auspices of the Ministry of the Interior by Journaux Officiels, 26 rue Desaix, 75 Paris 15, France, 1971. 263 listings, 134 pages.

GERMANY. *Deutsche Stiftungen fur Wissenschaft, Bildung and Kultur.* Published by Nomos Verlagegesellschaft, Baden-Baden, Germany, 1969. 629 listings, 428 pages.

INTERNATIONAL. *International Foundation Directory.* Gale Research Co., Book Tower, Detroit, MI 48226. 686 listings for 45 countries in North America, Europe, South America, Japan, and parts of Asia. 1979.

LATIN AMERICA. *Philanthropic Foundations in Latin America.* Russell Sage Foundation, 230 Park Avenue, New York, N.Y. 10017, 1968. 215 pages.

NEW ZEALAND. *Directory of Philanthropic Trusts.* New Zealand Council for Educational Research, P.O. Box 3237, Wellington 1, New Zealand, 1964. 59 listings, 68 pages, available free upon request.

RICHARDS, MARILYN W. *European Funding Resources for Women in Development Projects.* Secretariat for Women in Development, New TransCentury Foundation, 1789 Columbia Road, N.W., Washington, D.C. 20009, 1979.

SWEDEN. *Svenska Kulturfonder.* P. A. Norstedt & Soners forlag, Stockholm, Sweden, 1970. 700 listings (approximately), 288 pages.

UNITED KINGDOM. *Directory of Grant-Making Trusts.* National Council of Social Services, 26 Bedford Square, London, WCIB 3HU, England, 1971. 2,000 listings (approximately) and 854 pages.

QUIZ

Answer true or false.

1. There are three basic types of foundations: private family, community, and corporate.
2. A foundation must give away all its yearly income, according to current IRS regulations.
3. The total number of foundations in this country is increasing.
4. The primary reason proposals are rejected by foundations is because they do not meet the foundations' stated priorities.
5. Standard and Poor's *Foundation Record* gives a complete listing of the nation's largest foundations.
6. The federal government is second only to foundations in amount of dollars given to support nonprofit organizations.
7. About 10 percent of foundations in this country have 90 percent of the available staff and handle almost 90 percent of the dollars.

8. *The Foundation Directory* is good for information on small family foundations.

9. In most cases, you cannot get foundation funds unless you identify yourself with an established nonprofit organization.

10. The best method of seeking foundation funds is to send well-prepared letters to fifteen or twenty of your top choices.

Chapter 8

SPECIAL EVENTS

All the other chapters have dealt with basically low-profile fund raising approaches, involving a limited number of people and a great deal of interpersonal bargaining. This chapter deals with participative fund raising: the bazaars, luncheons, bingos, garage sales, fun runs, auctions, theatre parties, raffles and charity balls; all of which involve a lot of people and a lot of fun. There are as many special event fund raisers as there are people to dream them up.

Special event fund raising is an excellent way not only to raise money but also to increase participation in your organization, identify new members, and gain some community public relations for your ideas. The trick is to use your friends and volunteers to put on an event at the lowest possible cost, attracting as many people as possible while making money for your organization. In short, it is a high-work, low-capital venture.

Every organization should have at least one special event built into its fund raising strategy. Funds raised through these events are unrestricted and can be applied toward any portion of the organization's budget. Special event fund raisers are an excellent technique for both new grassroots organizations who need start-up funds and existing organizations who need an annual boost or emergency cash to meet the month-end payroll. Bingo is proof of the success of special event fund raisers for established institutions.

Because the most successful special event fund raisers often approximate controlled chaos, there is need to organize carefully. This chapter will help you through the Special Event Checklist and sample worksheets. Someone will need to be in charge of planning the event, carefully laying out the who, what, how, when, and where of each task. Someone must organize the volunteers and be in charge of publicity, and someone must keep the books. Remember to start small. If you haven't planned a special event before, you are more likely to get a repeat performance by your volunteers and participants if they have an initial success. The best way to gain experience is to work as a volunteer in a fund raiser in your city. Good luck, and above all, have fun doing it.

SOME SPECIAL EVENTS

Ad Book—Local merchants pay to advertise your program, bulletin, or catalog.

Auctions—Arts and crafts, memorabilia, farm auction, antiques, television auction.

Bazaars and Fairs—Antique and art fairs, flea markets, school carnivals, neighborhood festivals, ethnic festivals. Include many booths (plants, books, clothes, cakes, candies, toys, games, and white elephants).

Dances and Parties—Holiday dances and Halloween parties, dinner dances, the annual dance, gala parties, bingos, and casino nights.

Door-to-Door—Sales or solicitation (need license in most areas).

Concerts, Theatre, and Symphony Events

Fashion Shows and Tours—Many businesses will assist you and provide the location and refreshments.

Food and Dining—Coffee, luncheon, dollar-a-plate potluck supper, clambake, pancake dinner, community barbeque, watermelon party, winterfest, international foods dinner, wine and cheese-tasting party.

Lectures—Celebrity or athletic lecture.

Movies—Films, documentaries, cartoon festivals.

Raffles—Cash or prize raffle, raffle a month.

Special event fund raisers.
Source: *The State News*, East Lansing, MI 48824, and *The Lansing State Journal*, Lansing, MI 48919.

Sales—Rummage, garage sale, used books, materials your organization has developed (books, cookbooks, self-help materials, or other items).

Sports Events—Marathons (walk-a-thons, swim-a-thons, etc.); fun runs; cross-country ski races; tennis, racquetball, volleyball, and golf tournaments; celebrities vs the slobs softball game.

Sweepstakes and Lotteries—These have always been popular but heavily regulated fund raisers. Several states now operate daily lotteries. Michigan and Massachusetts now have systems which allow nonprofit organizations to raise money by selling lottery tickets.

Telethon—Television or radio. Phone-a-thons have become quite popular also.

NOTE: You can combine events and always include concessions along with your main event.

Don't forget to include handicappers in these and all events by making sure your event is accessible.

SPECIAL EVENT FUND RAISERS

THE LAS VEGAS NIGHT

A casino night involves gambling, entertainment and refreshments, all presented with Las Vegas-style razzle-dazzle. These are especially popular in states that do not have legalized gambling because they offer people a chance to gamble for fun. Some will get merchandise prizes too. They appeal to organizations because they raise a lot of money and provide so many different ways to volunteer that everyone can star at some part.

One format for a casino night is to sell advance tickets which admit the players, give them a set amount of play money ($20,000), and serve as door prize tickets. The customers then get to gamble with their play money. Get the standard games and instructions from a carvinal supplier. The games—roulette, craps, black jack, etc.—are staffed by your most vivacious members, who can explain the games simply and encourage people to play.

Each customer gets an instruction sheet that explains the games and a list of the prizes with "prices" listed in play money. Get the prizes from your carnival supplier and solicit others, like dinners at local restaurants and gift certificates to local stores. Successful gamblers can trade in their play money for prizes if they want to leave early. If they lose all their play money they can get more at the "currency exchange" where you sell play money for real money. Unlike illegal gambling, you are neither taking nor paying out real money, and you don't need to worry about the dealers skimming.

The secret of success is getting the gamblers to stay and gamble all night. So keep the best prizes like the stereo, TV, trip to Hawaii, or ten-speed bike for an auction at the end. Then the best gamblers will bid for the top prizes with their winnings. Also, hold the door prize drawing at midnight.

In addition to the gambling, you can sell food and drinks. Have lots of waiters and waitresses to serve the gamblers drinks. Sell food in other rooms decorated as cafés. A school makes a great setting for a Las Vegas night because you can gamble in the gym, and run different shows and restaurants in other rooms. Sometimes groups combine the food and entertainment, like having the German band in the room with the beer and bratwurst and the Dixieland band in the room with the oyster bar. Or you can use the auditorium and put on a full-tilt musical production with singing and dancing. Sell the refreshments separately and include the entertainment in the ticket price.

Line up some celebrities to take a shift running one of the games for you, too. It is fun for the celebrities and the crowd. In addition it will build up your repeat customers, if they think they can get lucky with the senator or the second baseman dealing.

Source: Joan Flanagan, *The Grass Roots Fundraising Book*. Washington, D.C.: The Youth Project, 1977.

SILENT AUCTION

You can run a silent auction any time you get something that is very appealing and unusual. You may get more money by auctioning it off then by simply marking a price on it. Good candidates would be an excellent handmade quilt or valuable antique.

Simply place the item on display with a note about its history and value. Put a poster next to it with a marker and a beginning (minimum) bid on the top. Then each bidder puts a higher bid under the last:

	Handmade Quilt
Minimum bid:	$100
Mark Twain:	120
Martha Washington:	130
Will Rogers:	140
Etc.	

Post the final time for bids, say 4 p.m. Make a final announcement at 3:45 that it is your last chance to bid on the quilt. At 4 p.m. whoever has the highest bid gets the quilt.

Source: Joan Flanagan, *The Grass Roots Fundraising Book.* Washington, D.C.: The Youth Project, 1977.

THE MARATHON

The walk-a-thons and other fundraising marathons raise money from a lot of people pledging to pay the participants money per output. For example, in a walk-a-thon, walkers will collect pledges for contributions from 10 cents to $1 for every mile they walk. The volunteers can walk, ride bikes, swim, dance, or play volleyball. Obviously the marathons offer tremendous publicity opportunities in addition to high income.

To be successful you have to recruit a large number of young people through school networks to solicit the pledges and do the walking. Then a professional staff takes over to do the billing and collecting of the pledges. Walk-a-thons work best for issues that appeal to young people, like environmental issues, or for issues promoted by the leaders young people respect, such as the hunger walks organized by popular church leaders.

To find out how to run a marathon, ask local fundraisers who use the technique....

Source: Joan Flanagan, *The Grass Roots Fundraising Book.* Washington, D.C.: The Youth Project, 1977.

SPECIAL EVENT
FUND RAISER CHECKLIST

☐ Keep cost down, especially for your first fund raiser.

☐ Maximize participation.

Involve all your people in planning and carrying out the special event.

Example: a luncheon can be planned by two people; casino night involves many more.

☐ Have fun.

Controlled chaos.

Do what your people enjoy, and participation will increase.

☐ Start small.

If you have never organized a special event, begin with something simple like a coffee, garage sale, or raffle.

Go to a special event as a participant or volunteer.

☐ Be successful.

Since your special event is public relations for your organization, you want it to be a success.

A luncheon can fail; a potluck dinner never has.

NOTE: Always consider concessions at all your events. They are a refreshing convenience and add to profits.

PLANNING THE ACTUAL EVENT

BUDGET

Determine the amount you need to raise.

Itemize expenses—materials, supplies, rental, and so on.

Estimate income—you should make two estimates, one high and one low. The low estimate is designed to give you the maximum loss possible.

Profit—actual income minus expenses gives you the amount you made on the event.

FORMAL CONCERNS

You may need to take out a short-term insurance policy to cover your event. Check with your insurance agent.

Written permission, waivers, and so on can save you last minute embarrassment on the use of the dance hall or gym.

STAFFING

Set up a committee structure to handle the various aspects of your special event; for example, for a fun run the considerations are course layout, volunteers, equipment, awards, entry forms, refreshments, public relations.

Determine maximum number of volunteers needed.

Identify and recruit volunteers.

Assign individual responsibilities.

SUPPLIES AND MATERIALS

Determine supplies and materials down to the last thumbtack.

Keep these to a minimum.

Have supplies donated when possible.

SCHEDULING

Set a date that won't conflict with other fund raisers which will draw on the same participants. Check your calendar of community events.

Be weather-wise. Don't plan a garage sale for February in Minnesota. Also, avoid holidays such as Mother's Day, Thanksgiving, and Christmas unless your event coincides with the holiday, such as a Christmas tree sale.

Make a time chart of your event, listing who, what, how, when, and where.

PUBLICITY

Publicity brings out the participants.

A special event will only be as successful as its publicity.

Plan this feature well in advance.

Develop a multimodal approach using flyers, posters, letters, radio, television, newspapers, and word of mouth.

CLOSING ACTIVITIES

Sweep the floor, straighten the chairs, turn off the lights, return the equipment.

Pay the bills.

Thank everyone involved, particularly your volunteers.

NOTE: There are many excellent sources on how to organize a special event. They vary widely in price and specificity. Joan Flanagan's *Grass Roots Fundraising Book* is the best one on the market. The book is poorly distributed but can be ordered directly from the Youth Project, 1555 Connecticut Avenue, N.W., Washington, D.C. 20036.

FUNDING STRATEGY PORTFOLIO

EXERCISE 1

Criticize one special event fund raiser which has occurred in the area recently.

EXERCISE 2

Work as a volunteer on a fund raiser in your city.

SAMPLE CHART FOR GETTING SUPPLIES

SHOPPER'S NAME: E. Scrooge PHONE: 787-1000 EVENT: Christmas Party DATE: December 18, 1977

ITEM	ALREADY HAVE	STORE	PRICE	ADVANTAGES	WHO CAN DONATE	WHO CAN LEND	WHO CAN PICK UP & **RETURN**
Receipts	500						Bob
Hall					American Legion		
Door Prize					J's Jewelry Store		Fred
Raffle Drum						St. Bastion's	Sister Margaret
Sound System		S Sound	$15 Rent	will bill			Ralph
Liquor		A	$40	will deliver			
(all on consignment)		B	$45	free ice			Mike
		C	$50	closest; open til 4 am			Mike
Coffee Maker		D	$30				Sallie
		E	$30	Repair in store			Sallie

Source: Joan Flanagan, *The Grass Roots Fundraising Book*. The Youth Project, 1555 Connecticut Avenue, N.W., Washington, D.C. 20036.

SAMPLE REPORT — URBAN CHURCH
1976 FALL YEAR

BOOTH	REVENUE AND CONTRIBUTIONS	EXPENSES	PROFIT (LOSS)	PERCENT PROFIT
Boutique (resale clothes)	$202	$——	$202	100
Kids' Games	128	50	78	61
Baked Goods	515	—	515	100
Beer	116	108	8	7
Handicrafts	1,136	155	981	86
Candles	99	—	99	100
Herbs	163	—	163	100
Barbecue	236	70	166	70
Dinner and Cocktails	1,549	942	607	39
Flea Market (resale items)	913	—	913	100
Ice Cream	91	38	53	58
Silent Movies	1	—	1	100
Raffle	507	—	507	100
Gate (publicity expenses)	344	63	281	81
Melodrama	56	51	5	9
Pony Rides	56	145	(89)	(Loss)
Total	$6,112	$1,622	$4,490	73%

May, 1979

Dear Auction Activator:

Throughout the short history of Auctions, it has become evident that volunteers either make or break their success. Never was that more obvious than several weeks ago when the volunteers literally carried off the successful completion of our second GREAT TV/23 AUCTION.

From the most menial task to the glamorous on-air auctioneer, our volunteers gave their very best. It was heartwarming to see how wholeheartedly each and every one put his/her very best into whatever job they sought or were asked to do.

Our phone-power gals who came each day, during the cold, gray days of winter, our go-getters and the Jaycees who must have taken a crash course in city maps and environs in order to seek out the "booty" so necessary for the Auction. And then the week of the Auction, when innumerable pairs of hands and legs appeared miraculously, (thanks to the determination of Carol Welch and her sore ear) to take on any and all tasks so willingly and so tenaciously without a thought of personal gain or recognition.

It was beautiful and impressive to those of Staff who were, by and large, being paid to do what you people were so enthusiastically and efficiently accomplishing. I sincerely hope you are all feeling the gut-level satisfaction of knowing you have done the job so well and that all those hours of grinding, literally back-breaking in some instances, labor are what made the Auction such a great success.

Thank you. And remember, now that you are all "pros" we will expect you back next year to lead us on to further glory!

Sincerely,

Barbara Sutton
Auction Coordinator

BS:gm

WKAR-TV/ MICHIGAN STATE UNIVERSITY / EAST LANSING, MICHIGAN 48824

(517) 355-2300

Saying "thank you."

EXCERISE 3
List three special events which would be suitable for your organization's funding needs and indicate at what stage in your organization's development they would be most appropriate.

EXERCISE 4
Develop a plan for one special event to go in the portfolio. Be sure to itemize each task and indicate who is responsible for what, list materials needed, and include a time chart and projected budget.

BIBLIOGRAPHY

There is much written, jotted down, and in the heads of organizers out there on special event fund raising. Some are well-established events; others suggest uniqueness and creativity. Here are some good references to help in planning your event.

ALTER, JOANNE. "101 Sure Fire Fund-Raising Ideas." *Family Circle Magazine*, Reprint Department, 488 Madison Avenue, New York, N.Y. 10022, October 1976.

COVER, NELSON. *Guide to Successful Phonathons.* CASE Publications, Box 298, Alexandria, Va. 22314, 1980.

FLANAGAN, JOAN. *The Grass Roots Fundraising Book: How to Raise Money in Your Community.* The Youth Project, 1555 Connecticut Avenue, N.W., Washington, D.C. 20036, 1977.

Good Cents—Every Kid's Guide to Making Money. Boston: Houghton Mifflin Co., 1974.

How to Raise Money for Community Action. Scholarship, Education and Defense Fund for Racial Equality (SEDFRE), One Penn Plaza, New York, N.Y. 10001, 1970.

KNOWLES, HELEN K. *How to Succeed in Fund-Raising Today.* The Bond Wheelwright Co., Porter's Landing, Freeport, ME. 04032, 1975.

LIEBERT, EDWIN R., and BERNICE E. SHELDON. *Handbook of Special Events for Non-Profit Organizations: Tested Ideas for Fund-Raising and Special Events.* Taft Products, Inc., 1000 Vermont Avenue, Washington, D.C. 20005, 1974.

MANDEL, ABBY EVARTS. *It's for Your Benefit.* Smith College, Northhampton, Mass. 01063, 1975.

Money Raising Ideas for Exchange Clubs. The National Exchange Club, Central Avenue, Toledo, Ohio 43606, 1979.

MUSSELMAN, VIRGINIA. *Money Raising Activities for Community Groups.* New York: Association Press, 1969.

Shaking the Money Tree. League of Woman Voters Education Fund, 1730 M Street, N.W., Washington, D.C. 20036, 1969.

SHERIDAN, PHILIP G. *Fundraising For The Small Organization.* Philadelphia: J. B. Lippincott Co., 1968.

"Special Events Fund-Raising." *The Grantsmanship Center,* 1031 South Grand Avenue, Los Angeles, Cal. 90015. Reprint No. 201.

TENBRUNSEL, THOMAS W. "Non-Profit Organizations, Recession, Volunteers and Fundraising." *Volunteer Administration,* Vol. XIII, No. 4 (Winter 1980-81), pp. 1-3.

Ways and Means Handbook—A Chairman's Guide to Money Making Projects. The Sperry and Hutchinson Co., Consumer Relations, P.O. Box 935, Fort Worth, Tex. 76101, 1964.

WHEELER, ALICE M. *Fundraising Projects of Symphony Women's Association.* American Symphony Orchestra League, Inc., P.O. Box 66, Vienna, Va. 22180, 1975.

QUIZ

Answer true or false.

1. A special event fund raiser is a good way to raise start-up money for your fledgling organization.
2. Special events fund raising is most successful when it approximates controlled chaos.
3. Special events fund raising is not for the more established organizations in a community.
4. Holding a special event is a good way to gain publicity for your organization.
5. Special events fund raising is an excellent way to raise unrestricted dollars for your organization.
6. An emergency special event fund raiser has helped more than one agency out of its end-of-the-month payroll problem.
7. There is not much need to develop a budget and time chart for a special event fund raiser since it is just people getting together to have fun.
8. It is not really necessary to acknowledge volunteers for their work since they work for free.

9. Special event fund raisers typically require a lot of front-end money and minimal personal involvement from staff and volunteers.

10. If you are worried about whether your special event will be successful or not, you should consider having a potluck supper rather than a luncheon.

Index

DATE DU